A GUIDED TOUR THROUGH HISTORY

Vicksburg

MIKE SIGALAS

With an introduction by James C. Bradford

travel

Guilford, Connecticut

An imprint of Globe Pequot Press

Maps by Trailhead Graphics © Morris Book Publishing, LLC
Historical PopOut map and historical interior map on p. 20 courtesy of the Library of
Congress.

All photographs by Mike Sigalas, except for the following: Photos on pp. iii, iv, and
27 courtesy of Shutterstock; photos on pp. 9, 12, 13, 14, 15, 16, 20, 21, 61, and 77
courtesy of the Library of Congress; photos on pp. 10, 18, 19, 24, 30, 35, 75, and 78
courtesy of Noah Sigalas; photo on p. 29 courtesy of the Vicksburg National Military
Park; photo on p. 67 courtesy of the National Park Service.

Library of Congress Cataloging-in-Publication Data

Sigalas, Mike.
  Vicksburg : a guided tour through history / Mike Sigalas ; with an introduction by
James C. Bradford.
     p. cm.
  Includes bibliographical references and index.
   ISBN 978-0-7627-5332-1
   1. Vicksburg National Military Park (Miss.)—Guidebooks. 2. Vicksburg (Miss.)—Histo-
ry—Siege, 1863. I. Title.

   E475.27.S55 2010
   973.7'344—dc22

                                                                          2009029530
Printed in China
10 9 8 7 6 5 4 3 2 1

All the information in this guidebook is subject to change. We recommend that
you call ahead to obtain current information before traveling. All restaurants are
open daily for breakfast, lunch, and dinner, unless otherwise noted.

Contents

Acknowledgments

The author owes special thanks for the invaluable help of historian-author Terry Winschel of Vicksburg National Military Park; for the gracious hospitality of Bill Seratt and the rest of the team at the Vicksburg Convention and Visitors Bureau; and for the contributions of Dixie Jackson Weaver on Frederick Grant and the Vicksburg Caves.

Introduction
by JAMES C. BRADFORD

Vicksburg, a key strong point on the Mississippi River, was the focus of the drive by Union forces aimed at subdividing the Confederacy and opening the Mississippi River to Union navigation. Surrender of the "Gibraltar of the Confederacy" on July 4, 1863, marked the end of the decisive campaign in the Civil War's Western Theater. General Ulysses S. Grant's successful prosecution of the campaign led to his promotion to command of all Union armies.

From the start of the Civil War, Union leaders had pursued a three-part strategy, the "Anaconda Plan," designed to defeat the Confederacy. That strategy called for the U.S. Army and Navy to apply consistent pressure on the Confederacy, ultimately crushing the South like its namesake, the Amazon constrictor, strangled its prey. Operationally, the Anaconda Plan called for (1) a naval blockade of the entire coast of the Confederacy that would stop Southern exports and prevent the importation of foreign goods; (2) the exerting of constant pressure against Confederate armies, particularly

A barge passes beneath the Mississippi River Bridge, linking Mississippi and Louisiana.

in Virginia; and (3) a subdivision of the South that would disrupt its economy and prevent the movement of armies and war supplies from one region to another.

Union forces commanded by Major General Ulysses S. Grant initiated the first attempt to cut the Confederacy in half during the spring of 1862 by driving south through Tennessee and, in conjunction with the navy, captured Forts Henry (February 6, 1862) and Donelson (February 16, 1862). Striking south toward the railroad junction at Corinth, Mississippi, Grant's advance was checked at Shiloh Church near Pittsburg Landing on the Tennessee River (April 6–7, 1862).

While this campaign unfolded, Union forces to the west began the process of opening the Mississippi River. The northern end of the Confederate defenses was anchored on Island No. 10, so named because it was the tenth island south of the juncture of the Ohio and Mississippi Rivers; it was a natural strongpoint at the head of a double bend in the Mississippi. Union troops, supported by navy gunboats, probed the seemingly impregnable Confederate position until Brigadier General John Pope hit on the idea of having two gunboats run past Island No. 10 to provide cover for his troops to cross the river below the fort, so that they could circle back and attack the Confederates from the rear. The operation succeeded, and on April 7, the same day as the battle at Shiloh, Major General John McCown surrendered Island No. 10 including 7,000 troops and 158 pieces of artillery. Eleven days later U.S. Navy ships opened a weeklong bombardment of Forts Jackson and St. Philip south of New Orleans. On April 23 Flag Officer David G. Farragut ran his fleet, minus the mortar boats left to continue their bombardment, past the forts and proceeded upriver to New Orleans and occupied the city on April 24.

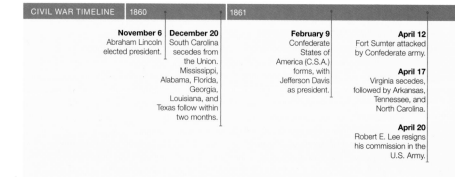

Operations in the west now focused on Vicksburg. President Abraham Lincoln stated that "The war can never be brought to a close until that key is in our pocket," and, on October 25, 1862, Grant was ordered to make the city the target of his operations. Only eleven days earlier, Lieutenant General John C. Pemberton had been placed in command of Confederate troops in western Mississippi and ordered to hold Vicksburg at all costs and

The Mississippi State flag is one of the last in the U.S. to pay homage to the Confederacy's Stars and Bars.

prevent a link-up of Union naval forces to the north and south. A horseshoe bend in the river forced vessels to slow as they passed the city, making them easy targets for the Confederate batteries mounted along the city's high bluffs.

Grant initially planned a two-pronged attack against the city. He would personally lead 40,000 troops south along the Mississippi Central Railroad that ran from Memphis to Jackson. Using the railway for logistical support, he planned to penetrate central Mississippi then swing west to approach Vicksburg between the numerous small rivers, swamps, and bayous that protected the city against approach from the north and the sharp ravines that hampered approaches from the south. Meanwhile, his subordinate,

1862

July 21
First Battle of Bull Run (First Manassas)

November 1
President Lincoln appoints George B. McClellan general-in-chief of the U.S. armed forces.

January 31
Lincoln issues General War Order No. 1, calling for U.S. forces to advance by February 22.

February 6
Major General Ulysses S. Grant captures Fort Henry in Tennessee, and Fort Donelson ten days later.

Major General William T. Sherman, and 32,000 troops would move by boat down the Mississippi from Memphis, land north of Vicksburg, and attack from there.

But once the attack was initiated little went according to plan. First, 3,500 Confederate cavalry under the command of Major General Earl Van Dorn swept around Grant's advancing army, overwhelmed the 15,000-man garrison Grant had left to guard his supply base at Holly Springs, and burned the supplies there on December 20. Meanwhile other Confederate cavalrymen, commanded by Brigadier General Nathan Bedford Forrest, ranged north of Holly Springs, tearing up 60 miles of track that connected that town to Columbus, Kentucky, the place where Union supplies were transferred from riverboats to the railroad.

Sherman's men did not fare better. After leaving their boats on December 26 and struggling though swamps, on December 29 they attacked Confederate positions at Chickasaw Bluffs, northeast of Vicksburg, where they were repulsed, suffering 1,700 casualties while inflicting fewer than 200 casualties on their opponents. Their defeat, the vulnerability of rail lines to cavalry attack, and the example of successful joint operations with the navy earlier in 1862, led Grant to develop a new strategy for capturing Vicksburg.

First he moved his headquarters to Young's Point, just north of Vicksburg, on January 20. From there he directed expeditions designed to probe Confederate defenses. In February, Brigadier General Leonard F. Ross led an expedition along the Yazoo, Coldwater, and Tallahatchee rivers designed to flank defenses at Vicksburg and attack the city from the rear. The Yazoo Expedition ended on March 16 when Ross concluded that the Confederate position at Fort Pemberton, located at the confluence of the Tallahatchie and

1862

April 6 and 7	May 31	June 1	July 11	August 29–30
Confederates surprise Grant at Shiloh; 23,000 men are killed or wounded in the fighting.	Battle of Seven Pines: Confederate General Joseph Johnston attacks near Richmond and is seriously wounded.	With Johnston incapacitated, General Robert E. Lee assumes command of the Army of Northern Virginia.	Lincoln appoints his Commander of the Department of the Tennessee General Henry Halleck general-in-chief of the entire Union Army; General U.S. Grant takes over most of his former command.	Second Manassas: Lieutenant General James Longstreet and General Stonewall Jackson defeat the Union Army of the Potomac.
April 24 Flag Officer David Farragut leads seventeen Union ships to take New Orleans.		**June 25–July 1** The Seven Days Battle near Richmond; McClellan begins withdrawal from the South.		

The Mississippi and Yazoo Rivers are still important shipping channels today.

Yalobusha rivers, was too strong to attack and withdrew his men. A week later, on March 24, General Sherman abandoned a similar plan to approach Vicksburg via Steele's Bayou. These failures convinced Grant to forget about attacking Vicksburg from the north.

In late January a Confederate supply steamer came out of the Red River, turned upstream, ran past the few Union guns sited along the Mississippi, and delivered its cargo to Vicksburg. Grant knew that such deliveries had to be stopped, and the success of the steamer in eluding fire from Union

1863

September 4–9
The Confederate army invades Harper's Ferry, West Virginia.

September 17
Battle of Antietam: 26,000 men are dead or wounded by day's end; Lee withdraws to Virginia.

September 22
Lincoln issues a preliminary Emancipation Proclamation.

November 7
Lincoln replaces McClellan with Major General Ambrose Burnside.

December 13
Burnside is roundly defeated at Fredericksburg, losing more than 12,000 men to the Confederate army's 5,300.

January 1
Lincoln issues the formal Emancipation Proclamation, freeing all slaves in Confederate territories.

January 25
Lincoln replaces Burnside with Major General Joseph Hooker.

batteries convinced him that Federal vessels could run past the Confederate guns at Vicksburg. Just after dawn on February 2 the Union gunboat *Queen of the West* ran past Vicksburg, suffered only three hits from the batteries in the north of the city, set fire to a Confederate riverboat, then ran past the guns south of the city, taking only twelve additional hits, none of which inflicted serious damage.

Based on these experiences, Grant decided to duplicate the strategy employed at Island No. 10. He would send units of his army across to the west bank of the Mississippi with orders to circle well south of Vicksburg and rendezvous with navy gunboats, which would transport them back across the river. On the night of April 16 Grant ordered a flotilla of transports and gunboats to run downstream past the guns of Vicksburg, losing only one transport in the process. To distract Confederate attention from these movements, Grant dispatched Colonel Benjamin Grierson and 1,700 cavalrymen on a raid into Mississippi on April 17.

Two weeks later, Captain David D. Porter began ferrying Grant and his main army across the river at Bruinsburg. By the end of April, now back in Mississippi, Grant decided against moving directly against Vicksburg. Instead he headed east toward the state capital at Jackson hoping to lure Confederate Lieutenant General John C. Pemberton out of the defenses at Vicksburg so he could engage him in the open field rather than have to either assault Pemberton's strong positions around Vicksburg or to lay siege to the city for an extended time. Pemberton did not take the bait and Grant, after defeating smaller Confederate contingents at Port Gibson (May 1) and Raymond (May 12), occupied Jackson, the capital of Mississippi, on May 14.

1863

May 1-4
Lee defeats Hooker at Chancellorsville; Stonewall Jackson is mortally wounded and dies on May 10.

May 18
Following successive defeats at Fort Gibson, Raymond, Champion Hill, and Big Black River Bridge, Major Lieutenant-General John C. Pemberton's army flees inside the defensive works around Vicksburg.

May 19
Grant orders his men to assault the Vicksburg works. Only Major General William T. Sherman's corps is in place (on the Union right) when the assault begins. The Confederates thwart the assault.

May 22
Grant orders a 10 a.m. assault all along the Confederate lines. Repulsed, Grant decides to stop the attack but orders a second attack at 2:00 p.m. after receiving encouraging words from Major General John McClernand on the Union left. The 2:00 p.m. assault is equally bloody and futile.

May 23
Grant reconciles himself to a protracted siege. Work begins on a series of approach trenches (saps) towards the Confederate lines.

May 27
River batteries and a gun emplacement at Fort Hill on the north end of the Confederate defenses sink the U.S. ironclad *Cincinnati*.

Leaving Sherman and a portion of his army in Jackson, Grant and the rest struck westward toward Vicksburg. General Joseph Johnston, overall Confederate commander in the area, ordered Pemberton to move out from Vicksburg and coordinate an attack with his forces against Grant. Pemberton reluctantly complied with the order and sallied forth with 22,000 of his men to meet Grant's army, which had turned west from Jackson and was advancing toward Vicksburg. The two met at Champion's Hill, a 75-foot-high knoll that lay astride the path of two of Grant's divisions. In the ensuing engagement Grant lost 410 killed and 1,844 wounded to Pemberton's losses of 381 killed and 1,800 wounded. More importantly, Pemberton's force lost much of their cohesion with several units, including a division under Major General William W. Loring, the commander whose troops had turned back the Yazoo Expedition the previous March, refusing to return to Vicksburg, opting instead to try to link up with Johnston's army. The next day Pemberton lost another 1,700 men while crossing the Big Black River.

Grant aggressively pursued Pemberton's men and launched his first assault on the earthworks at Vicksburg on May 19, hoping to penetrate them before the Confederates could reorganize their defenses. The attack was repulsed, as was a larger one (on May 22) against a 3-mile-long stretch of the Confederate lines that resulted in 3,200 Union casualties against fewer than 500 for the defenders.

These failures convinced Grant that any assault would fail so he opted to initiate siege operations. Confederates had spent nearly seven months constructing a virtually impregnable system of interconnected redans, redoubts, and lunettes. These earthenworks of varying shapes and design formed an arc—like a backwards capital "C"—around Vicksburg, known to residents

June 3
Lee's men begin their march into Pennsylvania.

June 18
Grant charges McClernand with insubordination and has him removed from command, replacing him with General Edward Ord.

June 25–26
Union General John A. Logan's men explode a tunnel dug beneath the 3rd Louisiana Redan at Vicksburg. The resulting "battle of the crater" ends after 48 bloody hours with yet another repulse of the Federals.

June 28
Lincoln replaces Hooker with Major General George Meade.

July 1
The Union blows up the 3rd Louisiana Redan a second time, but dares not follow up with a charge of infantry.

July 1–3
Meade defeats Lee at Gettysburg, turning the tide of the war.

July 3
Pemberton and Grant meet and discuss surrender. After a deadlock, their subordinates help the commanders agree to terms.

July 4
Confederate troops stack their arms and Union troops march in to occupy Vicksburg.

July 4
A six-week siege at Vicksburg ends with Confederate surrender to Grant.

as the Queen City of the Bluffs, that began on the Mississippi River north of the city and ended on the river to the south. Designed to take full advantage of the bluffs, ravines, gullies, and swamps that ringed Vicksburg, the strong points were linked by a system of trenches and rifle pits.

So formidable were the defenses that Grant believed it necessary to execute a classic five-step siege involving investment, bombardment, construction of parallel and approach trenches, and a breaching of the defenses followed by a final assault. He added to these a sixth element: the digging of tunnels under Confederate lines in which kegs of black powder were ignited in an attempt to blow holes in the enemy's lines. This ploy failed and as Union soldiers dug in, their emplacements came to mirror those of their Confederate counterparts. The result was a six-week ordeal that inflicted intense suffering on the residents of Vicksburg as well as on the Confederate defenders. Grant knew that having to feed the civilians would deplete Confederate stores and thus shorten the siege, so he refused to let even women and children leave the city. By the end of May, Grant had nearly 70,000 troops, twice the 30,000 Confederate defenders.

The surrender of Vicksburg and that of Port Hudson five days later gave the Union effective control of the Mississippi River, cut off Texas, Arkansas, and most of Louisiana from the rest of the Confederacy, and led President Lincoln to proclaim that "the Father of Waters again goes unvexed to the sea." Food and other supplies from the trans-Mississippi Confederacy could no longer be transported to armies in the east. Control of the river conveyed on the Union the opportunity to penetrate its tributaries and attack deep into the Confederacy in campaigns exemplified by the Red River Campaign of 1864.

1863

1864

September 19–20
Defeated at Chickamauga, the Union Army of the Cumberland becomes trapped in Chattanooga.

October 16
Lincoln appoints Grant as commander of the West.

November 23–25
At Chattanooga, the Union army finally defeats the Confederates under General Braxton Bragg.

The Seige of Vicksburg, July 4, 1863

It was these results, which Union General-in-Chief Henry W. Halleck foresaw when he wrote. "In my opinion, the opening of the Mississippi River will be of more use to us than the capture of forty Richmonds." Indeed, the surrender of Vicksburg coincided with the Battle of Gettysburg, a Union victory that marked

March 9
Lincoln appoints Grant general-in-chief.

May 5–6 and 8–12
Battles in Wilderness and Spotsylvania turn the war in the Union's favor; Major General William Sherman begins a march to Atlanta with 100,000 men.

June 3
Grant makes an error that costs 7,000 Union soldiers their lives at Cold Harbor, Virginia.

June 15
The nine-month Union siege of Petersburg begins with the Union army surrounding Confederates.

July 22
Major General James McPherson is killed by skirmishers outside Atlanta.

The statue of Grant on horseback shows him riding Kangaroo, originally given to him as a joke after the battle of Shiloh.

the turning point of the Civil War in the east. The dual defeats at Vicksburg and Gettysburg struck a severe blow to Confederate morale. As one Southern leader stated, "Yesterday we rode on the pinnacle of success—today absolute ruin seems to be our portion. The Confederacy totters to its destruction."

September 2
Sherman captures Atlanta.

November 8
Lincoln is reelected president, ensuring continuance of the Union war effort.

November 15
Sherman's Army begins its devastating March to the Sea.

December 5–16
55,000 Union troops defeat Major General John Hood's army at Nashville.

December 21
Sherman reaches Savannah and the sea, leaving a swath of destruction and bitter Southerners in his wake.

January 31
The Thirteenth Amendment officially abolishes slavery.

Modern visitors find it difficult to appreciate how Vicksburg once commanded the Mississippi River because that mighty waterway changed course during the early twentieth century and now bends 5 miles south of where it did in 1863, leaving only the unimpressive Yazoo River Diversionary Canal to flow past the city. On the other hand, it is relatively easy to visualize the siege of Vicksburg and attacks from the east because so many trenches and earthworks remain. As with several other Civil War battlefields, preservation began with the establishment of a National Military Cemetery. The one at Vicksburg was established by Congress in 1866 for the reburial of over 17,000 Union dead, 95 percent of them unidentified.

When veterans of the 24th Iowa Infantry met in Vicksburg for a reunion in 1895, they were distressed to find the scene of battle and the siege marked only by a single inscribed cannon preserved at the site of the surrender meeting between Grant and Pembertion. Iowa veteran John F. Merry began organizing the Vicksburg National Military Park Association. Incorporated in November 1895, the group lobbied Congress to appropriate funds to preserve the important sites in the area. In February 1899 Congress established the Vicksburg National Military Park. Returning veterans were able to identify the locations where their units had fought and several state governments erected monuments to mark the spots. The 1,325 monuments range from simple plaques to the Ohio State Memorial, a Greco-Roman temple surmounted by a dome. In 1933 the War Department transferred responsibility for the park to the National Park Service, which ceded a portion of its land to the city of Vicksburg in return for the city's agreement to close the local roads that bisected the park.

March 25	April 2	May
Lee's forces in Petersburg attack Grant's army, and are defeated in four hours.	Lee evacuates Petersburg. Richmond is evacuated.	The C.S.A. reunites with the United States.
	April 9 Lee surrenders to Grant at Appomattox.	
	April 14 Confederate-leaning actor John Wilkes Booth shoots Lincoln at Ford's Theatre in Washington. Lincoln dies early the next morning.	
	April 18 Johnston surrenders to Sherman in North Carolina.	

Key Participants

Officers of the Union

Major General Ulysses S. Grant (Commander of the US Army of the Tennessee) The newly-appointed head of the Army of the Tennessee, Grant had been effectively relieved of command after his failure to prepare his troops had contributed to the loss of over a thousand men at the battle of Shiloh in April, 1862. As he began his operations against Vicksburg in December of 1863, Grant knew his support back in Washington was fragile. His desperation to achieve victory at Vicksburg as quickly as possible caused him to order three futile and devastatingly bloody assaults on the well-defended Confederate works.

Major General John A. Logan A fiery orator and one of the Union's most capable politician-officers, John A. Logan held down the left of McPherson's corps. His men fought in every major encounter during the forty-seven days of the siege: the assaults on June 19 and 22, as well as the Battle of the Crater on June 25, 1863. Because of their courage and sacrifice, Grant allowed Logan's surviving men the honor of leading the march into the city after Vicksburg's fall on July 4.

Major General John A. McClernand, (Commander of the XIII Corps) A politician turned general, McClernand, having served under Grant at Fort Donelson and Shiloh in 1862, convinced President Abraham Lincoln and Secretary of War Edwin Stanton to allow him to raise and lead a separate force of men to capture the Confederate bastion at Vicksburg. General Ulysses S. Grant and his Army of the Tennessee were already trying to do the same thing, and McClernand's arrival in Mississippi in January 1863 caused friction between the two men. Although Grant absorbed McClernand's army into his own, he never trusted the politician, and when McClernand wrote a letter praising his own corps's valor in the attacks of May 22, 1863—suggesting that they had only failed because of Grant's lack of timely support—Grant removed McClernand for insubordination. On June 18, midway through the siege, McClernand was replaced by General Edward Ord. Lincoln's aid, John Hay, described McClernand as "a vain, irritable, overbearing, exacting man who is possessed of the monomania that it was a mere clerical error which placed Grant's name and not his in the Commission of the Lieutenant General."

Major General James B. McPherson (Commander of the XVII Corps) James B. McPherson graduated from West Point at the top of his class in 1853. A skilled engineer, he rose quickly under Grant and commanded the XVII Corps throughout the Vicksburg campaign. During the siege, McPherson's troops held the center of the Union line, where they engaged in some of the hottest fighting during the failed assault of May 22 and in the gratuitous Battle of the Crater on June 25 and

26. During the surrender talks on July 3, McPherson and his old West Point classmate Major General John S. Bowen successfully worked out the terms of surrender after Grant and Confederate Commander James Pemberton hit a stalemate in negotiations. A year later, McPherson was killed while fleeing Confederate pickets outside Atlanta.

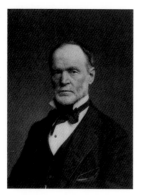

Major General William Tecumseh Sherman (Commander of the XV Corps) Sherman had a reputation in the Eastern papers as a depressive naysayer prone to overestimating the amount of men he needed to oppose the enemy. His friendship with and loyalty to Grant saved his military career. His corps held the Union right during the siege, and after May 23, 1863, Sherman himself led expeditions to the Union rear to keep Confederate General Joseph E. Johnston's army of relief from attempting to rescue Pemberton's men. Although Sherman had initially opposed Grant's plan of marching at Vicksburg from the south, Grant wrote of him in his memoirs, "His untiring energy and great efficiency during the campaign entitle him to a full share of all the credit due for its success. He could not have done more if the plan had been his own."

Officers of the Confederacy

Major General John S. Bowen One of Confederate Commander John C. Pemberton's ablest generals was an old prewar friend of Grant's from Missouri. His men chiefly served as reserves during the siege of Vicksburg, rushing forward whenever the Union threatened to create a breach in the lines. Although desperately ill with dysentery, Bowen's brinkmanship on July 3 saved the surrender negotiations between Grant and Pemberton. Dysentery took Bowen's life just nine days after Vicksburg's fall.

General Joseph E. Johnston (Commander of the C.S.A. Army of Relief) The highest-ranking U.S. Army officer to resign at the start of the Civil War, Johnston was still recovering from serious gunshot and shrapnel wounds received in early June 1862 at the Battle of Seven Pines when he was hurriedly sent back into service by Confederate President Jefferson Davis in mid-May 1863, with orders to take command of all Confederate troops in the Western Theater of the war—including John C. Pemberton's Army of Vicksburg. His main objective: keep Vicksburg from falling into Union hands.

Grant later wrote that he respected and feared Johnston more than any other Confederate general, but Johnston arrived at nearby Jackson, Mississippi, only in time to find himself cut off from Pemberton's men by Grant's army. He spent the 47 days of the siege attempting to build a new "army of relief" in Jackson to battle Grant and possibly—at Jefferson Davis's behest—attempt a rescue of Pemberton's army in Vicksburg. By the time he finally marched his troops west toward Vicksburg, Pemberton had surrendered the city.

Nonetheless, for a man who never set foot within 20 miles of Vicksburg during the entire campaign, Johnston had a large effect on the actions of both armies. Grant's fear of an attack on his rear by Johnston gave him cause for trying to end the siege through violent assaults on May 19, 22, and

June 25, 1863. Pemberton and his army believed Johnston was on his way, and for this reason, they held on even when it became clear they were running out of supplies. The siege did not end until Pemberton and his generals lost faith that Johnston would rescue them.

Lieutenant General John C. Pemberton (Commander of the C.S.A. Army of Vicksburg)
Pennsylvania-born Lieutenant General John C. Pemberton arrived as Commander of the Army of Vicksburg in 1862 only after losing the confidence of troops and civilians at his former command in Charleston, South Carolina. A capable administrator and engineer, Pemberton had no field command experience. During the siege of Vicksburg, he toiled under a pair of conflicting orders: President Jefferson Davis had told him to hold Vicksburg at all costs; General Joseph Eggleston Johnston, his direct superior, had told him to evacuate the city, save his army, and ride east to join Eggleston's men and fight Grant. His obstinacy in the July 3 surrender interview with Grant nearly caused the bloodshed to continue, but in the end resulted in more favorable concessions for his men. Although President Jefferson Davis continued to support Pemberton, most Confederates blamed him for Vicksburg's fall, and he was never given command of another Confederate army.

Vicksburg National Military Park: A Historical Tour

Before You Begin: Park Visitor Center

Stop inside the visitor center, just inside the park's main entrance. Outside you'll see a display of the various cannons used on both sides of the siege. Check out the re-created parapet. Just inside the doors, speak to the people manning the visitor center booth. They can provide you with helpful maps of Vicksburg.

The reconstructed parapet outside the center illustrates a sample section that might have belonged to any of the various forts along the Confederate defensive lines. Most Southern soldiers spent the forty-seven-day siege behind walls much like these. The idea was to have a floor deep enough in which to stand without risking sniper

"The war history of Vicksburg . . . is full of variety, full of incident, full of the picturesque. Vicksburg held out longer than any other important river-town, and saw warfare in all its phases, both land and water—the siege, the mine, the assault, the repulse, the bombardment, sickness, captivity, famine."
—Mark Twain, *Life on the Mississippi*, 1883

Model parapet, visitor center

Vicksburg National Military Park entrance

fire, but with embrasures cut into the walls through which artillerists and sharpshooters could fire at attacking enemies.

Be sure to watch the 18-minute film *In Memory of Men,* playing every half hour from 8:00 a.m. to 4:30 p.m. It will provide you with a quick overview of the Vicksburg campaign. The re-created Vicksburg bomb shelter display is well worth a look, as is the exhibit telling the story of the Corps d'Afrique and its historic defense of Milliken's Bend against Texan raiders who were trying to relieve their besieged fellow Confederates in Vicksburg. Although barely trained, the African-American troops fought fiercely, proving—to some, anyway— that "colored" troops could indeed do more than dig trenches.

Why Vicksburg?

From the day he was appointed commander of the Union Army of the Tennessee, Major General Ulysses S. Grant knew he needed to capture the Confederate city of Vicksburg. At the start of the Civil War, General Winfield Scott had urged, in what came to be known as his Anaconda Plan, the immediate blockade of all Southern ports on the Atlantic and Gulf Coasts, and "a powerful movement down the Mississippi to the ocean."

Blocking the South's coastal ports would separate the Confederacy from possible allies or trading partners abroad, and Scott's "powerful movement" to recapture control of the Mississippi would deprive the South of the produce of its own farms and tanneries in the West. Its soldiers and civilians would go hungry, and—as Scott said—the Union

Vicksburg

"Vicksburg is the nail head that holds the South's two halves together."

—C.S.A. President Jefferson Davis

could "bring them to terms with less bloodshed than by any other plan."

To rule the Mississippi, however, the Union needed to capture Vicksburg. Its location just below the convergence of several other rivers made it a sort of naval crossroads town. It was located just below Desoto Bend, a hairpin turn so sharp it forced ships heading downriver to reverse engines and slow to a crawl just as they came under the shadow of the high bluffs on which the "Hill City" was built.

These 200- to 300-foot bluffs provided numerous places where gun batteries could fire down on passing ships with virtual impunity, particularly since most guns could not be angled high enough to reach the bluffs. In Vicksburg, the Confederacy had a veritable Southern Gibraltar—which became the nickname for the previously unassuming delta town.

It was for these reasons that President Abraham Lincoln, in a discussion with his war strategists, is famously said to have stood before a map of the region and pointed straight at Vicksburg. "See what a lot of land these fellows hold of which Vicksburg is the key. . . . The war can never be brought to a close until that key is in our pocket." (The statue *The War Council*, in the visitor center's museum, portrays Lincoln, Grant, and Secretary of War Edwin Stanton as Lincoln looks at a map and makes this pronouncement. (The artist took poetic license here: Lincoln and Grant didn't meet until after Vicksburg.)

Grant knew that Lincoln was right. If he could capture Vicksburg, he would control the entire river, and could use the river to launch expeditions eastward, deep into the heart of the Confederacy.

"Mississippians don't know, and refuse to learn, how to surrender to an enemy."
—**Vicksburg Commander James L. Autry, May 18, 1862**

The Milliken's Bend Memorial

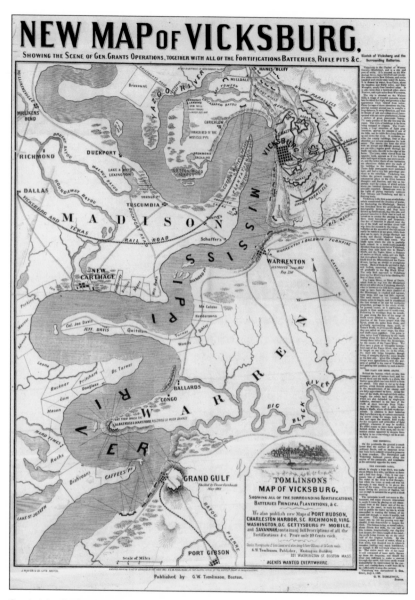

Created shortly after the end of the Vicksburg Campaign, this map shows the movements of Grant's troops, as well as the Confederate fortifications they faced.

APRIL 18th, 1863: The Vicksburg Campaign Comes . . . to Vicksburg

General Ulysses S. Grant figured he'd rather face the Rebels while they were exhausted, disorganized, and discouraged by their string of defeats beginning with Port Gibson on May 3 and on through the Battle of Big Black River Bridge on May 17. His men had significant momentum after a week's worth of victories. And so, eager to finish the job he'd started in 1862, Grant ordered an attack for the morning of May 19. He felt certain that the disillusioned Southerners "would not make much effort to hold Vicksburg."

Grant was wrong, and the master tactician's miscalculation would cost hundreds of men their lives.

"Vicksburg is worth seeing, and a glance will tell you more than reams of paper why it took us six months to take the place."
—General William T. Sherman to his brother, July 28, 1863

General Ulysses S. Grant

Tour Stop 1: The Shirley House, Illinois Memorial, Logan's Approach, and the 3rd Louisiana Redan

As you drive between and the visitor center and our first stop, you'll continue for a time behind the Union trenches to your left. After the road sharply jogs west you'll catch your first glimpse of both the Shirley House and the most striking of all the state monuments here at Vicksburg: the Illinois State Memorial. Park in the spaces provided in front of the monument.

The Shirley House

James and Adeline Shirley, who owned this house, were pro-Union. In fact, most people in the Vicksburg area had been Unionists right up until January 7, 1861, when their votes failed to stop secession from the Union at the Mississippi State Secession Convention in Jackson. As did many Unionists across the South, once their state formally seceded, most residents of Vicksburg enthusiastically supported the Confederacy.

But not the Shirleys. Native New Englanders, they moved here with James Jr., James's son from his first marriage. They purchased this home and the surrounding farmland in 1851. James Sr. established a thriving law practice in Vicksburg and the family farm prospered. The Shirleys purchased twenty-five slaves to work their land and serve in their house, and Adeline bore three children: Frederick, Alice, and Quincy.

In May of 1863, hearing reports of the battles in and near Jackson, 69-year-old James Shirley, Sr.

headed down Jackson Road on foot towards Clinton, where young Alice attended a girls' school. Knowing the dangers inherent to young girls amid rampaging armies, James wanted to bring her back home to safety. Ironically, of course, for the next forty-seven days, this house would be one of the most dangerous addresses in all of Mississippi.

By the time Confederate soldiers, bloodied and dispirited from two weeks of defeat, stumbled past the Shirley House on May 18, 1863, James and Alice had not yet returned from Clinton. Hearing cannons in the distance, Adeline set her slaves to work digging a cave down in the ravine to your right. The Confederates had sent men to burn down any building that might provide cover for the approaching Northerners, but when a young Rebel came to the Shirley House, Adeline Shirley refused to leave the house. The Confederate soldier refused to burn her alive, but he had orders to obey, and the Yankees were fast approaching. Finally, the desperate Rebel put his torch to the side of the roof—but was shot down before it caught fire.

According to Alice Shirley, the soldier crawled under "some nearby planks" and died, and was buried the next day in the yard.

The Shirley House may not have been aflame, but Adeline, James Jr., and their servants nonetheless found themselves surrounded by a kind of hell between the retreating Confederates and the Federals who were firing at them.

Necessity being the mother of invention, Mother Shirley tied a white sheet to a broom handle and ordered a slave to wave it from the front balcony. It worked: The Union army ceased fire.

"Walk right in; it's a splendid place. I was shot in the leg here yesterday."
—Colonel Jasper Maltby of the 45th Illinois, welcoming another officer to the Shirley House, quoted by Sergeant Wilbur F. Crummer, 45th Illinois

A Guided Tour through History

The Shirley House, known simply as "the white house" to most Union soldiers, is the only man-made structure from the siege still standing.

Nonetheless, advancing Union troops soon surrounded the house, and while the Shirleys were noncombatants, the Yankees weren't, and the Confederates opened fire on them. The Shirleys and their servants hid inside their fireplace, which kept them safe from the gunfire.

Eventually, the entire hillside to the right of the Shirley house would be honeycombed with small personal caves, or bombsafes, where General Logan's men—who did more than their share of sap digging in the later days of the siege—could rest and sleep, relatively safe from Rebel fire.

The house itself, during the siege, would be used as an observation point and a headquarters of the 45th Illinois. In his 1915 autobiography *With Grant at Fort Donelson, Shiloh, and Vicksburg: And an Appreciation of General U. S. Grant*, Sergeant Wilbur F. Crummer of the 45th Illinois Volunteers recounted how General Grant and other commanders often visited the house to get a good look at what they called "Fort Hill"—the 3rd Louisiana Redan—some 350 yards directly opposite the house, and to check the progress of Logan's approach.

After the surrender, the Shirleys never returned to their house. Badly damaged by shot and shell, it was converted into a Union smallpox hospital after the siege, and then abandoned completely. Alice Shirley Eaton and her husband sold it to the Federal government, along with 60 surrounding acres, in 1900. Alice's parents, James and Adeline Shirley, lie in graves behind the house. Their headstone proudly notes their Yankee birthplaces in New Hampshire and Massachusetts.

The Illinois Memorial

If you visit no other memorial at Vicksburg, visit this one. Its forty-seven steps—one for each day of the siege—lead to an open domed structure wherein you can see, all round you, the names of

Missouri Regiments fought for both armies at Vicksburg. This frieze memorializes the state's Union troops.

every Illinois soldier known to have fought in the Vicksburg campaign—36,325 in all.

The two nameplates that most guides like to point out are that of William Dent Grant—Ulysses's thirteen-year-old son, who was here largely as an observer, but who is listed under "Staff" for the Army of the Tennessee, and the 95th Illinois Company G's Private Albert D.J. Cashier—in reality, a woman named Jennie Hodges who enlisted, fought, and lived for over forty-five years as a male veteran before her true gender was discovered.

Those are the popular stories. The most impressive thing about the monument, however, is the sheer number of names inscribed on its walls.

If possible, stand here on an uncrowded day and contemplate the silent testimonies to the 36,325 men (and woman) who sacrificed their youths, and often their lives, in defense of the Union.

If you pause for only one state memorial here, make it the Illinois.

From the bottom step of the Illinois Memorial look to your left along the park road back at the Shirley House. The park road between these two places is paved over the former Jackson Road. Just past the Shirley House, the park road veers sharply left, keeping in line with the Union's trenches, but if you were to continue straight ahead on the unpaved road, you would be following the route of the old Jackson Road.

Logan's Approach

Facing the front of the Shirley House, the depression in the earth to your left is part of the remains of Logan's Approach.

Of the thirteen sap or trench approaches dug by Grant's men toward the Confederate line, most famous is that dug by Major General John A. Logan's men. Starting from the ravine to the east of the Shirley House, this six-foot-deep, eight-foot-wide trench was the channel up which poured the men of the 45th Illinois and 23rd Indiana on June 25, to what came to be known as the Battle of the Crater. The sap began in the ravine to the right of the Shirley House, and zigzagged from side to side, generally along the Old Jackson Road, until it nearly reached the base of the 3rd Louisiana Redan, at the top of the hill facing the Shirley House.

Illinois Memorial

"We are now approaching with pick and shovel."
—General William T. Sherman, to his brother Senator John Sherman, May 29, 1863

Mr. Logan's Conversion, from Moderate to Radical

Before he was a major general, Congressman John A. Logan of Illinois campaigned for fellow Illinois Democrat Stephen Douglas in 1860, convinced that Lincoln's election would lead southern states to secede. On February 5, 1861, with six states already seceded, Logan delivered a call for compromise and union. His twenty-page speech was published and widely distributed.

Like Lincoln, Logan believed secession was constitutionally impossible, and both felt any civil war would be bloody and long. But they disagreed in where to lay the blame for the crisis. While Lincoln famously warned the southern states that "In your hands, my dissatisfied fellow countrymen, and not mine, is the momentous issue of civil war," Logan felt that the "meddling," "abolition agitation," and uncompromising attitude of radical anti-slavery Republicans was equally responsible for the crisis.

"[Southerners] are not our enemies," he reminded the Republicans, "but a part of our people." If these "kinsmen" were treated "with forbearance and moderation," Logan believed that the "revolting" states would voluntarily return from their "wanderings" on their own, without any need for bloodshed.

The alternative of forcing the states back into the Union at gunpoint would mean certain war. "The first blood shed," he prophesied, "will operate as a signal for fresh and more extensive slaughter; a dark veil of terror and death will cover our whole land."

Logan's speech was ultimately ineffective. When war broke out, he made good his promise to "go as far as any man" for the Union. As a Midwesterner, he knew about the importance of the Mississippi River to northern commerce. He electrified Unionists from the floor of the Senate when he proclaimed that before the United States allowed the Confederacy to control the Mississippi, "men of the Northwest would hew their way to the Gulf with their swords."

After fighting in Bull Run as a volunteer, Logan returned home to Illinois and formed the 31st Illinois Volunteer Infantry Regiment, and was named its colonel. By the time he reached Vicksburg, he was a brigadier general. The war turned Logan into a fierce northern partisan—and a resolute Republican. He was elected to the House of Representatives, where he helped lead the Radical Republican attempt to impeach Andrew Johnson. As founder and first president of the Grand Army of the Republic—a Union veterans group—he was instrumental in having Memorial Day named a national holiday. After election to the Senate, he ran unsuccessfully for U.S. vice president on a ticket headed by James G. Blaine. By 1886, the same year he died, his one-sided retelling of the Civil War and its causes, titled *The Great Conspiracy: Its Origin and History,* showed that the temperate, even-handed Logan had disappeared somewhere after Bull Run.

While back in 1861 Congressman Logan had scorned those who tried to label the South's secession as a mere "rebellion," when in fact it was a full-fledged revolution, in *The Great Conspiracy,* he used the word "rebellion" to describe the Confederacy no less than 262 times.

The 3rd Louisiana Redan Attack

To reach the next National Park Service (NPS) tour stop, simply walk or drive westward along the paved road past the Illinois Memorial. In doing so, you're following the path of the Old Jackson Road, the most heavily traveled access road into Vicksburg in 1863. Now follow the road southwest. You'll shortly pass a small clearing on the right with plaques identifying the site of Battery Hickenlooper, the first advanced battery made possible by the progress of the Logan Approach. Continue until you reach the third NPS tour stop: the Third Louisiana Redan.

The gravel road before you—the old Jackson Road, now used as a service road by the National Park Service—continues on between two earthen ridges. The high ridge to your right is all that remains of the southern wall of this redan, which pointed towards the Shirley House.

"The first consideration of all was—the troops believed they could carry the works in their front, and would not have worked so patiently in the trenches if they had not been allowed to try."
—**General Ulysses S. Grant, *Personal Memoirs of General U. S. Grant***

This map of the approach trenches and tunnels to the 3rd Louisiana Redan was drawn by their designer, Captain Andrew Hickenlooper, Chief engineer, XXVII Army Corps.

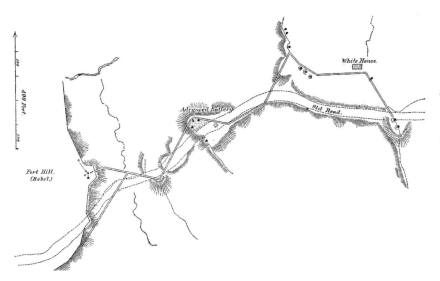

The 3rd Louisiana Redan from
Battery DeGolyer

Behind this wall, high above this road, Confederate sharpshooters kept anybody from approaching Jackson Road. But that didn't mean that nobody would try. After the failed assault on May 19, Grant let his men rest up and eat well for a couple of days, before sending them forward again on Friday, May 22, 1863. McClernand's men were deployed on the Union left, Sherman on the Union right, and McPherson's men would fight it out here in the center.

Major General John A. Logan assigned Brigadier General John E. Smith's 1st Brigade to assault the 3rd Louisiana Redan, while he assigned Brigadier General John D. Stevenson's 3rd Brigade the task of frontally assaulting the Great Redoubt, to the left of the Jackson Road.

The barrage of artillery, begun the night before, continued through the early morning. Sergeant Wilbur Crummer of the 45th Illinois, bivouacked in the ravine just east of the Shirley House, remembered "every piece of artillery was brought to bear on the works."

At 10 a.m., the 31st and 124th Illinois ran forward to the left of Jackson Road and hit their

"I am nearly reduced to the proper fighting weight."
—**Private Josiah Edwin Benton, 3rd Louisiana Volunteers, June 10, 1863, before being killed by a Union sniper.**

bellies, opening fire on the parapets to provide cover for the men of the 23rd Indiana, now jogging down Jackson Road four abreast, bayonets fixed, followed by the 20th Illinois.

When the 23rd got about 100 yards from the redan, taking heavy fire, it broke to the right of the road, allowing the 20th to move forward in its place. When the 23rd reached the foot of the redan, they realized that the ditch here was deeper than they had thought; the ladders the army had provided them for climbing the parapet walls were still several feet too short. Men dropped the ladders under the hail of killer Rebel fire pouring down from the tops of the redan walls.

Still on the Jackson Road, in the wake of the 23rd Indiana, the 20th Illinois advanced on the road close to the redan, angling left of the salient angle, and finding shelter on the slope of the ridge before the Confederate works.

And there they lay through the heat of the day. Grant decided to call off the attack, convinced that it was hopeless to proceed, but that afternoon, optimistic and somewhat misleading messages from McClernand led Grant to attempt a second wave of attacks, against his better judgment.

Thus, at 2:00 p.m. the 45th Illinois, under command of Major Luther H. Cowen, advanced on the road by the flank with fixed bayonets, supported by the 20th Ohio of the Second Brigade. The leading regiment advanced close to the salient angle of the redan, angled to the left and found shelter on the slope of the ridge immediately behind the already hunkered men of the 20th Illinois.

The tablet marking the spot where Cowen was killed leading his men was placed there by

"At ten o'clock we had orders to advance. The boys were expecting the order and were busy divesting themselves of watches, rings, pictures, and other keepsakes, which were being placed in the custody of the cooks, who were not expected to go into action. I never saw such a scene before, nor do I ever want to see it again. The instructions left with the keepsakes were varied. For instance, 'This watch I want you to send to my father if I never return'; 'I am going to Vicksburg, and if I do not get back just send these little trifles home, will you?' . . . Not a bit of sadness or fear appears in the talk or faces of the boys, but they thought it timely and proper to dispose of what they had accordingly."
—**Diary entry by Sergeant Osborn Oldroyd of the 20th Ohio Volunteers, May 22, 1863**

"It seems to me, in looking back, a wonder that anyone in that hot place was left to tell the story."
—**Sergeant Wilbur Crummer, 45th Illinois**

"About eleven o'clock came a signal for the entire line to charge upon the works of the enemy. Our boys were all ready, and in an instant leaped forward to find victory or defeat. The seventh Missouri took the lead with ladders, which they placed against the fort, and then gave way for others to scale them. Those who climbed to the top of the fort met cold steel."
—**Diary entry by Sergeant Osborn Oldroyd of the 20th Ohio Volunteers, May 22, 1863**

Sergeant Wilbur F. Crummer of the 45th Illinois Volunteers in 1902. He was beside Cowen when he fell. According to Crummer, Cowen had just shouted the command, "double quick," and the men had just reached the open space with the idea of going over the enemy's works, when Cowen fell, "having only taken a step or two."

At this point, with the regiment's major dead and the ranking captain unaware of the fact, the 45th Illinois kept jogging down Jackson Road until Crummer, first sergeant at the head of Company A, figured the men in the rear were far enough along the road to form in line of battle all along the southern wall of the parapet. Under heavy fire, and still awaiting the order to charge, the men from Illinois hit the ground just to the right of the road here, at the very foot of the redan. There, Crummer wrote, by "flattening one's self about as flat as a hard tack," the men were comparatively safe from the lethal blizzard of Rebel fire. Looking back down the road at where he presumed the 20th Ohio should soon come at the double quick, Crummer saw the dead and wounded—from both the 10 a.m. and 2:00 p.m. assaults—"lay thick over that stretch of 200 yards."

Finally, the ranking captain gave the order to charge. The 45th Illinois rose to their feet and charged up the hill, only to meet "a sweeping volley of musketry at short range, which mowed the men down in bunches." The few men who made it as far as the top of the parapet, Crummer wrote, "fell as fast as they climbed up."

Seeing the insanity of the assault, the 20th Ohio's officers did not order their men forward.

The blue placard here to the right of the road today boasts that both the 20th Illinois and the 45th Illinois "remained in the positions gained until the evening of the 23rd," but this is a euphemism. The Union men here had to remain—they were pinned down under Confederate fire, and unable to retreat.

After nightfall, Crummer and his comrades slipped off the slope beneath the 3rd Louisiana Redan, across Jackson Road, down the ravine, and back to their bivouac behind the Shirley House. Incredibly, beside Major Cowen, the 45th Illinois had sustained only two casualties, neither of them fatal. Seven Federal soldiers had died in the assault on the 3rd Louisiana Redan, with seventy-two men wounded. Two other men had simply disappeared.

That night, an exhausted Oldroyd recorded the day's events in his diary, concluding that the day had seen only "another day of bloody fight in vain, except for an increase of the knowledge which has been steadily growing lately, that a regular siege will be required to take Vicksburg."

The Battle of the Crater

From the blue sign marking the farthest advance of Smith's Brigade on May 23, continue just a few yards farther southwest on the old Jackson Road to the yellow interpretative sign reading "the mine explosion". Here, a month and two days after the senseless assaults of May 22nd, Grant tried another scheme to shorten the siege that only served to shorten the lives of many of its participants.

"Just after noon, the enemy sprung the mine beneath the Third Regiment, which they had been so long preparing."
—**Sergeant William H. Tunnard, 3rd Louisiana Volunteer Infantry**

In the face of the costly May 19 and 22 assaults, Grant announced that he planned to simply "outcamp the enemy," tightly sealing the siege lines around Vicksburg and waiting for the Confederates' food to run out. Although slow, this was a relatively bloodless way to take the city and capture Pemberton's army.

All Grant needed to take Vicksburg, it seemed, was time. But Grant didn't want to waste time— the heat of the summer was coming and his men would soon be savaged by heatstroke, dehydration, and malaria. He also wanted to avoid a rear attack by General Joseph E. Johnston's Army of Relief, which had grown from 5,000 to over 28,000 men since the respected Confederate officer had arrived in Jackson on the eve of Champion Hill.

Early on the afternoon of June 25, 1863, you would be looking directly at the high walls of the earthen 3rd Louisiana Redan. To your right, you can see two blue position tablets, two cannons pointed at you, and the back of several red signs marking Confederate positions.

The blue sign nearest you marks the far end of Logan's Approach, the sap trench dug by Logan's men all the way here from behind the Shirley House.

By June 15, Grant felt a little more secure with the Federals' position. He wrote to his father, "I have been so strongly reinforced that Johnston will have to come with a mighty host to drive me away."

And yet, while Grant claimed that he felt the fall of Vicksburg to be "[not] in the least doubtful," a long siege did not fit into his goals for the campaign year. He continued, "If, however, I could

have carried the place on the 22nd of last month,
I could by this time have made a campaign that
would have made the State of Mississippi almost
safe for a solitary horseman to ride over. As it is,
the enemy have a large army in it [Johnston's], and
the season has so far advanced that water will be
difficult to find for an army marching, besides the
dust and heat that must be encountered. The fall
of Vicksburg now will only result in the opening
of the Mississippi River and demoralization of the
enemy. I intended more from it."

Union siege cannons like these
pounded away at Southern
defenders daily.

> "What a terrible sacrifice it was to hold that little piece of ground. It probably was all right to have made the charge into the crater after the explosion and try to make a breech inside the enemy's lines, but it surely was a serious mistake, either of Gen. Grant or Gen. McPherson, to cause that crater to be held for over 48 hours with the loss of brave men every hour."
> —Sergeant Wilbur Crummer, 45th Illinois

While Grant went on to write his father that, looking back, he could "see no blunder committed," one of Grant's deadliest blunders of the Vicksburg campaign was yet to come. In fact, one of his best generals, John A. Logan, had men working around the clock, digging their way towards the foot of the 3rd Louisiana Redan, and the Battle of the Crater.

Of all the sap trenches underway in mid-June, Logan's Approach was the furthest forward. Here, at the nearer blue "position tablet" on your right, you see the spot where the sappers turned over their shovels to a team of miners from the 45th Illinois, led by Colonel Jasper Maltby.

These human moles, in only two days, burrowed forty feet beneath the bottom of the 3rd Louisiana Redan, and stuffed it with, literally, a ton of explosives.

The Confederates had guessed at their enemy's intent and sunk countershafts straight down, hoping to explode charges that would shake the otherwise perfect-for-tunneling loess soil into a useless mush that was impossible to tunnel through without extensive shoring.

> "Hand grenades . . . made sad havoc amongst my men, for, being in the crater of the exploded mine, the sides of which were covered by the men, scarcely a grenade was thrown without doing damage, and in most instances horribly mangling those they happened to strike."
> —Sergeant Wilbur Crummer, 45th Illinois

Meanwhile, other shovelers built up a secondary parapet wall further back inside the redan. In case the redan wall was somehow breached, the Southerners could fire at its invaders from behind this second parapet.

As the morning of May 25 turned to afternoon, the 1st Brigade of Logan's 3rd Division, 17th Corps, shuffled shoulder to shoulder, four abreast down Logan's Approach, with the 45th Illinois at the head of the column. The men halted short of the tunnel entrance, and waited.

At 3:30, the redan's northeast corner exploded in a fountain of churning earth and human flesh 150 feet high. Before the last clods had returned to earth, the 45th Illinois had rushed into the 15-foot-deep, 30-foot-wide crater. Rather than rushing up the other side and into the Confederate works, however, the Federals found themselves staring at the Confederates' second, fall-back parapet, behind which stood a number of very hostile Louisiana infantrymen, flanked on either side by boys from Mississippi and Missouri.

The Battle of the Crater had begun. The Confederates charged over the inner parapet to chase out the Yankees, only to meet a blast of musket fire that sent some scurrying back over the parapet wall, and some to their graves. The Federals fired from behind the western rim of the crater—where the blue position tablet between the cannons stands, and eventually brought in a cypress log with fire holes drilled in it to fire behind. As the Yanks placed the log, however, the Confederates blasted it with a cannon, severely wounding Colonel Maltby of the 45th Illinois.

Despite the importance of breaking through the Confederate lines, the North could only put so many men in the crater at a time. Thus, the Battle of the Crater, fierce as it was, was limited by logistics to two Union regiments at a time. When the men grew weary of fighting and their guns overheated, one detail would replace the other.

After forty-eight hours of gunfire, grenade lobbing, and hand-to-hand combat, Grant gave up the fight, withdrawing the final Union troops from what had come to be known as "Fort Hell," on June 26 at—ironically enough—quitting time, 5:00 p.m.

"My God! They're killing my bravest men in that hole."
—Major General John A. Logan

A Guided Tour through History

"As we went into the crater, they met us with a terrible volley of musketry, but on the boys went, up and over the embankment with a cheer, the enemy falling back a few paces to an inner or second line of breastworks, where are placed cannon loaded with grape and canister, and these cannon belched forth their death-dealing missiles, . . . the line wavers, staggers, and then falls back into the crater."
—Sergeant Wilbur Crummer, 45th Illinois Volunteers

Tour Stop 2: The Stockade Redan Attack Site

The May 19th Assault

Return to your vehicle, drive back to the Shirley House, and turn left onto Union Avenue. The next stop is 1.9 miles away.

Along the way we'll bypass NPS tour stop 4, Ransom's Gun Path. Continue on to the fifth NPS tour stop (our second), the Stockade Redan.

You are now moving through the Union trenches. Not far past Ransom's Gun Path, you've left McPherson's Corps and entered the land held by William Tecumseh Sherman's XV Corps.

You'll find the marker for NPS tour stop 5 on your left. Park here.

A little past the pullout is Graveyard Road, which cuts across the one-way Park Loop (making it a good place to cut the tour short if you want to head off to lunch and return later). Graveyard Road was named for the obvious reason. But the graveyard comes later. Now, imagine that it is May 1863, and it's your job to somehow penetrate the Confederate lines here. Ahead of you, at the point on Graveyard Road where today the ground on the left rises above the road, stands the 17-foot-high earthen Stockade Redan. The redan forms a salient, or 60-degree angle here, with one wall continuing leftward, southwest and parallel to the road you've just driven, the other side dropping back due northwest, parallel to the Graveyard Road for some distance before you reach the wooden stockade—a wall of poplar logs with a gate—for which the Stockade Redan complex was named.

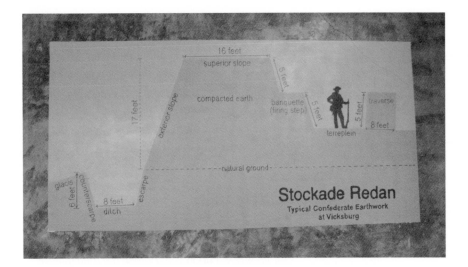

Stockade Redan

Typical Confederate Earthwork
at Vicksburg

This sign shows the design of the Stockade Redan.

If you wanted to try to batter down the stockade gate, you'd first have to reach the salient—with the men on the left and right walls firing at you, and then run the half-gauntlet alongside the right wall, past dozens of firing sharpshooters.

An attempt to storm the stockade gate itself would be suicide. Even Sherman and Grant—who were quite prodigal with other men's lives here on May 19 and 22—didn't attempt it.

Instead, Sherman tried to overwhelm the Stockade Redan itself, sending men straight up the parapet walls all along the redan. Again, imagine it is May 19, 1863, and you're part of the 54th Ohio or 55th Illinois, sent charging toward the redan from the area where you're currently standing.

Of course, all the trees and most of the grass are gone. You must march across a veritable moonscape into enemy fire, down the slope before you and then up the opposite slope, to the foot of the redan.

And there's more: The slope beneath the redan is covered with abatis—felled trees with sharpened branches bunched together to form a man-made briar patch up to 200 feet thick. As you claw your way through this, sharpshooters pour fire down at you from less than 50 yards away.

But imagine that, despite all this, you emerge from the abatis intact—or at least, still mobile—and charge up to the brow of the hill. As you get to within a dozen yards of the redan you are gratefully now protected from frontal fire by the height and width of the wall itself—some 16 feet thick at the top, making it impossible for musketeers to fire straight down upon you. Rather, the men in front of you take this opportunity to reload and wait for your head to appear atop the parapet while the men on your left—where the redan ends and the wall angles due south—open up at you with volleys of enfilading fire.

As minié balls whistle by you, you forge forward, telling yourself that determination and adrenaline will help you scale the redan's drastically steep, 17-foot-high incline—until you come across a grim surprise: All around the redan, the Rebels have dug a dry moat, 8 feet wide and 6 feet deep. The bottom six feet, nearly absolutely vertical, propel the practical height of the parapet to 23 feet.

On the morning of May 19, in preparation for just this sort of effort on the part of its infantry, the artillery of Sherman's army pounded away at the Stockade Redan, trying to knock out guns and soften Confederate defenses.

This was the impossible task facing the 83rd Indiana on the morning of May 19. Just north of Graveyard Road, Colonel Benjamin J. Spooner called his men into line and shouted, "This is the day of all days you are expected to show your valor and to show Jeff Davis that Indiana soldiers are not cowards."

At 2:00 p.m., at the signal of three artillery barrages fired in rapid succession, the men of the 54th Ohio and 55th Illinois headed forward from this spot, while the 83rd Indiana marched at double-quick for the same side of the redan—the south-west wall—from the far side of Graveyard Road. Looking down on the right of Graveyard Road, you would have seen the 1st Battalion, 13th U.S. Infantry running for the north wall. Behind them, the 116th Illinois, 113th Illinois, and 6th Missouri marched forward, six abreast, with orders to stay so close together that their elbows were touching.

Captain J.J. Kellogg of the 113th Illinois, in his memoirs of the Vicksburg Campaign, published fifty years later, remembered that first charge: "When the three rapid artillery discharges came we first stood up, then we scaled the log and pushed forward. On our immediate right was the 6th Missouri, and I being on the right of our regiment went in side by side with the men of their left."

Regimental Chaplain William Lovelace Foster of the 35th Mississippi Volunteer Infantry, C.S.A, watched in fear and terror. He later described the experience in a letter to his wife: *"A charge! a charge!* is whispered along the lines. . . . Can our men withstand the mighty concussion that awaits them? Under cover of a heavy artillery fire, they wind through the valley until they come in a short distance of our works. In perfect order, they form a solid body, six deep . . . they rush with flying banners—glittering arms."

One of those flying banners was held by Color Guard John Roberts of the 83rd Indiana. In his

"If anyone should fall in battle or get wounded, we were not even to turn him over or give him a drink of water until the battle was over."

—John Roberts, Color Guard, 83rd Indiana

account found in the Indiana Historical Society's Smith Memorial Library, he recalled passing the 13th Regulars and the 6th Missouri. These were some of Sherman's best regiments, and the 83rd Indiana were proving to be their equals—but then things turned bad in a hurry. Writes Roberts, "Here our regiment got somewhat demoralized, the color guards being nearly all shot down."

From Foster's point of view, however, the approaching Yankee regiments looked like an unkillable juggernaut: "On they come. Our cannon pours forth deadly grape into their ranks. They fill up the vacant gaps, without pausing a moment."

Meanwhile, Kellogg was beginning to suspect that keeping formation might be a problem: "A lieutenant on the left . . . was in his shirt sleeves and wore a white shirt; he and I went side by side for several steps, when he lunged forward upon the ground, and in the quick glance I gave him, I saw a circle of red forming on his shirt back."

When the Yanks had come within 70 yards of the parapets, all hell broke loose.

Foster narrates: "Now a thousand heads rise above. Above the earthworks, a thousand deadly guns are aimed—the whole lines are lighted up with continuous flash of firearms—every hill seems to be a burning smoking volcano."

Kellogg remembered: "The leaden hail from the enemy was absolutely blinding. The very sticks and chips scattered over the ground were jumping under the hot shower of rebel bullets."

And then, Kellogg and the other Federals reached the Confederates' abatis: "The rough and brush strewn ground over which we had to charge broke up our alignment badly, and every soldier of our command had to pick his own way forward as best he could without regard to touching elbows either to the right or left."

At some point "about two-thirds the way across the field," Kellogg and a corporal realized that they had gotten "considerably in advance" of the rest of their company and knelt down behind a fallen tree to wait for the others. A canister shot pierced the sole of the corporal's boot and lodged into his ankle. While Kellogg helped cut off the boot and dig out the ball, most of his company passed them by, and as he stood up to follow them saw only a handful of men he recognized, including his colonel and the regimental colors.

"I started towards our flag," he wrote, "but had gone only a few steps when one of the enemy's shells exploded in front of me, and when the smoke had lifted a little I saw that our regimental flag and the colonel had gone down."

Foster watched the mayhem on the Union line with some relief: "The enemies' solid columns reel—totter before this galling fire—like grass before the moving scythe they fall."

Kellogg himself didn't fall; he ran towards the Confederate works, looking for the surviving men of his company. Finally, in a shallow gulley just a "half-gunshot" from the Stockade Redan, Kellogg found seventeen men from his regiment "hugging the ground and keeping up a steady fire" on the redan: "I lay down with them at the upper end of the line where the cover was the least, because it was the only place left for me. . . . And there lying flat on our backs and loading our pieces in that position, with the merciless sun blistering our faces, we passed that day of dreadful fighting."

Although a few members of the 1st Battalion, 13th U.S. Infantry actually made it into the ditch

"After the enemy retired [and] the smoke had been dissipated, an awful scene was spread before the eyes of our brave men. The hillside was strewn with the dead—dying. . . . Thanks be to the Great Ruler of the Universe, Vicksburg is still safe."
—**William Lovelace Foster, Chaplain, 35th Mississippi Volunteer Infantry, C.S.A.**

A Guided Tour through History

and stabbed their regimental colors into the foot of the redan, there was no way they would get over the parapet walls. Sherman read the bloody writing on the walls and did not send his reserve units into the fray. The men trapped on the slope gave up the assault, hunkered down, and focused on survival.

By this time, Corporal Roberts had made it to within 50 yards of the Confederate works, planted his colors, and taken two loads of shot in the chest. He spent the afternoon sprawled in a ravine directly opposite the Stockade Redan's salient (now marked by a placement marker just to the right of Graveyard Road). Believing he was bleeding to death, Roberts crawled beside the body of the 83rd Indiana's Captain Mattellus Calvert, wanting to die by the side of his longtime captain.

Kellogg and the rest of Sherman's men who were pinned down under low ridges, or pressed against the inner wall of the ditch, waited until sundown. Then, emboldened by the cover of darkness and fearful that the Rebels would use the same darkness to burst out of the gate and kill or capture them, the Yanks withdrew, stepping over the bodies of the wounded and dead to their own lines. Through the night, recovery details pulled their wounded fellow enlistees—including color bearer John Roberts—to safety.

In the 83rd Indiana, forty-six men had been wounded and ten killed—including Calvert and a second captain. Across the whole of Sherman's lines, more than 150 men were dead or dying, and hundreds more were wounded. For the time being, Grant's irresistible force had been stopped, and at a heavy price to the would-be invaders.

Tour Stop 3: Thayer's Approach

To reach the next tour stop, drive 2.4 miles farther along Union Avenue and park at the sign for NPS tour stop 6, Thayer's Approach. Walk down the stairs to the right of the road. They'll lead you to a little tunnel beneath the road—now encased in brick, but in 1863 simply cut through the thick loess soil sans any shoring. This was the beginning of Thayer's Approach, the sap trench dug by the men of Brigadier General John M. Thayer, of Sherman's XV Corps Brigade.

Pass through the tunnel, beneath the road, and take a look at the topographical challenge that Thayer's men faced during the assault of May 22. Work on the various approach trenches all along the Confederate works began on May 23, and never ceased until the surrender. Although Logan's Approach was the most "successful" sap trench, Thayer's was surely the most challenging to dig. As you pass through the tunnel and down to the bottom of the ravine before you, the reason is clear— look at the steep, commanding bluffs ahead.

On June 22, Sherman sent men up this slope in a suicidal charge.

This tunnel beneath the park road was originally dug by Union troops trenching their way toward Fort Hill.

A general other than Grant—who liked to keep his boys busy with work—might have given Thayer's boys a pass on the sap detail, given the near-impossibility of ever hoping to reach the top. But then again, another general wouldn't have ordered his men to try to climb this same bluff in the face of thick enemy fire, as Grant (and Sherman, beneath him) had ordered Thayer's men to do on May 22.

The May 22 Attack

Remember the suicidal attack made by the Federal men at the Stockade Redan on May 22? As if that weren't overambitious enough, Grant and Sherman also ordered their men to attack the 26th Louisiana Redoubt, high atop the ridge in front of you.

Of course it failed. The Yanks were stopped by topography and enemy fire, in that order. Anyone could have foreseen this end, but Sherman and Grant—who incidentally, did not offer to make the charge themselves—sent fathers, sons, and husbands to their deaths, nonetheless, believing that a consistent pressure all along the Confederate lines would keep Pemberton's reserves from focusing on any one section.

Union Major Gustavious Lightfoot of the 12th Missouri could clearly read the situation realistically. Before the attack—which he would help lead—he broke out a box of cigars and offered them to the officers around him. Someone suggested that Lightfoot might want to hold onto a few stogies for a later date, at which Lightfoot replied, "Oh, take them. I will have no further use for cigars. This is my final smoke!"

And it was. With many others, Lightfoot was killed in the assaults of May 22, 1863, ordered by General Ulysses S. Grant and Corps Commander William T. Sherman. Grant and Sherman lived to smoke many another day.

Later, Thayer's men began digging a 6-foot-deep approach. His soldiers dug the tunnel beneath the road to avoid exposing themselves to Confederate fire while crossing the ridge on which it runs.

And so, after May 22, Thayer's approach began creeping forward from near the crest of a ridge, ran down the slope in front of you, and then up the opposite slope of the ravine, toward the ridge atop which 26th Louisiana Redan's salient sat. Cane fascines were laid across the roof of the trench, making it a virtual tunnel, reasonably safe from Confederate fire.

When the trench finally approached the salient at the top of the hill, the sappers heard enemy miners at work, digging countermines to blow up the sappers. The sap was stopped and Union miners began tunneling underneath the redan.

If you're in the mood (and condition) for a steep climb, head up the depression along the path of Thayer's Approach until you reach the end of Thayer's Approach marker. Had Pemberton not announced his intention to surrender on July 3, Grant planned, within a couple more days, to repeat the May 25 3rd Louisiana Redan mine explosion, simultaneously, at thirteen different locations along the Confederate works. An all-out assault on the Rebel defenses would have ensued, and hundreds if not a thousand or more men would have likely been killed.

Tour Stop 4: The U.S.S. *Cairo*

The U.S.S. *Cairo* was one of seven ironclad gunboats built to answer U.S. Military Commander Winfield Hancock Scott's call for a naval "push" down the Mississippi, through the Confederacy, and on to the Gulf of Mexico. The ships were built in Illinois and named in honor of towns along the upper Mississippi and Ohio rivers.

These ironclad side-wheelers packed a wallop—each held thirteen big cannon guns so large that if all of them on one side were fired simultaneously, it would tip the ship deeply towards the opposite side—exposing the unplated wooden hull to lumber-piercing rifle and artillery fire.

The "city class" gunboats were commissioned in January 1862. By May the *Cairo* had seen its first action at Plum Point. In June, it took a minor part in the battle of Memphis.

The *Cairo*'s skipper, Lieutenant Commander Thomas O. Selfridge Jr., would go on to have two more ships shot out from under him before the war was over—the U.S.S. *Conestoga* and the U.S.S. *Cumberland*. On the morning of December 12, 1862, Selfridge was all confidence. He had been given command of a small flotilla ordered up the Yazoo River to destroy batteries and clear the river of mines—then called "torpedoes."

Seven miles north of Vicksburg the flotilla came under attack, and Selfridge ordered the *Cairo*'s gunners to prepare to return fire. As the boat turned to point its mostly side-mounted cannons towards shore, two Confederate Acting Masters, Zedekiah McDaniel and Francis M. Ewing, hidden behind a blind, pushed a small plunger, sending electricity through insulated wires and through the water to a mine anchored beneath the *Cairo.*

USS *Cairo*

Two blasts ripped holes into the ship's wooden hull, wounding three men. Water poured in; crew members scampered up from the lower deck. Although the entire crew scrambled to safety, within twelve minutes the *Cairo* had sunk 36 feet beneath the Yazoo's surface—the first ship ever sunk by an electrically detonated torpedo. And there it would lie for the next 100 years, before the wreck was finally located, cut into thirds, and brought to the surface in September, 1964.

Although the star of the show here is the raised, walkable skeleton of the U.S.S. *Cairo,* the small museum nearby is certainly worth your while for its displays of artifacts pulled up from the wreck. Since the *Cairo* was vacated without warning, nearly everything on board—down to the crew members' personal items—was left behind to be found years later by the team that found and raised the boat.

Some simple but intriguing items here are the damage cones, which were used to plug small but sinking-inducing bullet holes in the ship's wooden hull. Unfortunately for Selfridge and his crew, the huge holes caused by the mine that doomed the *Cairo* were far too large for the damage cones to be of any use. In addition to the ship and the museum, the U.S.S. *Cairo* area features two timely amenities: public restrooms and picnic tables.

Tour Stop 5: Vicksburg National Cemetery

"The most beautiful of all the national cemeteries is here. . . . The grounds are nobly situated; being very high and commanding a wide prospect of land and river. They are tastefully laid out in broad terraces, with winding roads and paths; and there is profuse adornment in the way of semi-tropical shrubs and flowers, and in one part is a piece of native wild-wood, left just as it grew, and, therefore, perfect in its charm."

—**Mark Twain, Life on the Mississippi, 1883**

Of the nearly 17,000 Union soldiers buried here, about 13,000 are unknown—a significant statistic, given the fact that the Union won the campaign and dug these graves themselves. The problem was that the men who fought here in the late spring and early summer of 1863 wore no dog tags. Their names were stitched onto their blue wool coats, but in the balmy Mississippi weather, few men wore their coats into battle. When they were killed, many went unidentified.

Established in 1866, the cemetery is also the final resting place for veterans of the Spanish-American War, World Wars I and II, and the Korean War. Again, you won't find Confederates buried here—this land was set aside for men fighting for the United States military. To see the graves of men who died fighting for the Confederacy, you'll need to head over to Vicksburg's Cedar Hill Cemetery.

Tour Stop 6: Fort Hill

Here you've reached the northern end of that 9-mile, backward-C-shaped ring of Confederate defenses around Vicksburg. Because of its height and clear view of the hairpin Desoto Bend, where boats sailing down from points north had to reverse engines and maneuver slowly to make the turn, Fort Hill was also used as an observation post for the gun batteries stationed on the riverbanks below. It also served to protect the landward approach to Vicksburg along the Yazoo City Road.

Unlike the other Confederate fortifications on our tour, Fort Hill was never attacked from the rear—it was simply too high and imposing. However, the fort did take part in one of the last Confederate victories following the South's successful repulses of the assaults on May 22. Here on the morning of May 27, the detachment of men stationed here from the Tennessee Heavy Artillery Battery down on the river opened fire with their 3-inch rifles, joining in the barrage upon a flotilla of Union boats attempting to pass the Vicksburg guns, and sinking the U.S.S. *Cincinnati.*

The river from Fort Hill

"The Rebels generally know about where to shoot, and waste no ammunition."
—**Daniel Francis Kemp, survivor of the U.S.S. Cincinnati**

"Our stern was protected by . . . bales of hay. The pilothouse was also protected by hay. But this did us no good, but rather helped to sink us. For when we were struck below the water mark, the water came rushing in and it was impossible to keep her force by working the pumps. We attempted to move the hay, but the steel was flying around us so that we were obliged to desist."
—**Daniel Francis Kemp, crew member and survivor, U.S.S. Cincinnati, June 27, 1863**

The Sinking of the *Cincinnati*

In the late afternoon of May 27, a surviving member of the *Cincinnati*'s crew, Daniel Francis Kemp, wrote to his parents in New York from the deck of the flag ship *Black Hawk*, explaining that the nighttime running of the battery had been postponed for some reason so that the *Cincinnati* found itself steaming into the face of Fort Hill's guns—and those of the river batteries—in broad daylight at 10 a.m. on May 27.

Extra men were taken aboard to help man the ship's guns, Kemp explained. The batteries along the river and up at Fort Hill opened as soon as the *Cincinnati* rounded DeSoto Bend.

The boat continued floating downriver until it was "almost in front of the courthouse," at which point, Kemp wrote, "a shock came through the pilothouse, killing our pilot and wounding one of our quartermasters. One of our officers took the wheel, but after we had got rounded to and had got some distance within our lines, our rudder was shot away. This left us completely at the mercy of the batteries and as she was settling fast we were obliged to turn ashore. Our boat went down about a mile and a half from the rebel lines.

"The rebels kept up a continual fire for some time after we were sunk. A great many of our men were swimming ashore when a ball struck the bank throwing the mud many feet in the air and coming down and scattering in all directions. At this time a number of our men was sunk. I think our carpenter's mate was cut in two. I cannot be too thankful that I am safe."

Tour Stop 7: The Stockade Redan

Stop at NPS tour stop 10, the Stockade Redan. Now you're looking at the scene of the vicious Stockade Redan assaults on May 19 and 22 from the defenders' point of view. Just like the 157 men who were needlessly killed in the attack on the Stockade Redan on May 19, the Union men who attacked here on May 22 never had a chance against the entrenched Confederates.

Why attempt another attack after such a wretched failure on the 19th, especially when the increasingly reinforced siege lines could easily keep Pemberton locked up in Vicksburg until hunger drove him out? The idea for a widespread, second attack on Vicksburg was spawned by Grant's fixation on achieving a quick, clean completion of the city's capture. The longer Grant's men lay camped around Vicksburg, the more time Confederate General Joseph E. Johnston, 50 miles east, in Jackson, had to build up an opposing army. Once his men and not Pemberton's filled the Vicksburg defense works, Grant could then march out to defeat Johnston before he could cause trouble at the Union rear.

Reinforcements were on the way, of course—enough, in fact, so that by the time Johnston's army was large enough to even consider an assault on Grant's men—in early July—Grant had a full 77,000 men under his command. But Grant was in a hurry on May 22, still fatally underestimating the Rebels' strength and resolve, and anxious to finish up the fighting in his department before the hot summer weather set in and thirst and fever ravaged his fighting men.

"On the 20th of May, General Grant called the three corps commanders together. . . . We compared notes, and agreed that the assault of the day before had failed, by reason of the natural strength of the position, and because we were forced by the nature of the ground to limit our attacks to the strongest parts of the enemy's line, viz., where the three principal roads entered the city. . . . General Grant [ordered] for us to make all possible preparations for a renewed assault on the 22nd, simultaneously, at 10 a.m."

—General W. T. Sherman, Memoirs, 1890

Insofar as Grant and Sherman understood it, the May 19 assault had only failed due to a handful of easily surmountable problems. First, they knew that during the assault, Pemberton had effectively used Bowen's men to fill up any weak points in the Confederate line. Given that McClernand and McPherson hadn't been in position and hence couldn't apply much pressure on the Union left and right, Pemberton had been able to concentrate his reserves on the Union right, hence preventing Sherman's Corps from overpowering the supposedly "dispirited" Confederates.

The second mistake on May 19, Grant and Sherman decided, was their hasty reconnaissance of the Rebel works, which had allowed the attackers to be surprised by and left unprepared for the rough terrain and deep trenches encircling the Confederate works. Grant set his engineers to building ladders for scaling the walls from the trench bottoms.

The third thing that had gone wrong on May 19, according to the generals, was their men's inability to keep formation across the area's rough landscape—particularly once the companies reached the abatis on the slopes. If the men could stay in formation, and get to the foot of the works quickly enough—before too many of them were shot down—then, the two military schemers reasoned, with scaling ladders, the men could scamper up the parapets, dash across the top of the 16-foot-thick walls into the face of Rebel musket fire, and overpower the enemy before most of them—or, at least, not a strategically disabling number of them—were shot dead or otherwise rendered militarily useless.

To get his men to the parapets faster, Sherman decided to bypass the ravines and abatis and send his men barreling up Graveyard Road, four abreast, as a kind of human battering ram. Upon approaching the ditches in front of the salient, they would fan out into line of battle, jump into the ditch, plant their ladders, and scale their way to the top of the parapets.

As time was of the essence, only a couple of the rapidly manufactured wooden ladders were provided to each company, meaning that at any given point along the 3-mile front of the battle, a mere handful of men—if that—would be popping their heads above the far edge of the parapet at once, allowing the plentiful gunmen on the other side plenty of time to shoot them down, one after another.

The Forlorn Hope

It would be better, of course, if they could get more men over the wall at once than the ladders would allow, and the smartest place to do that would be at the salient, the angle where the Stockade Redan met the road. With this in mind, the Union's two military savants of the West really started thinking. What if an advance group could somehow fill in the 8-foot-wide, 6-foot-deep trench at the salient, reducing the parapet walls to an easily scalable 17 feet above the road?

It was a long shot. To fill up even a 3-foot-wide section of the ditch to make it flush with the surrounding ground, the advance group would have to dump 144 cubic feet of material in front of the salient. To accomplish this feat, motivated by what might best be described as homicidally reckless

"When soldiers enter upon a service that gives them only one chance in a hundred to survive it, the commander doesn't like to bear the responsibility of their deaths, and tenders them the precious privilege of voluntarily dying for their country."
—**Captain J.J. Kellogg, 113th Illinois**

"To the minute . . . 10 a.m. of May 22nd, the troops sprang to the assault. A small party . . . called a forlorn hope, provided with plank to cross the ditch, advanced at a run, up to the very ditch; the lines of infantry sprang from cover, and advanced rapidly in line of battle. . . . The rebel line, concealed by the parapet, showed no sign of unusual activity, but as our troops came in fair view, the enemy rose behind their parapet and poured a furious fire upon our lines."
—**General William T. Sherman**

optimism, Sherman decided that the advance group should contain just 150 men—meaning that if every man ran forward into the hail of bullets with one cubic foot of wood or stone or other debris, no more than six could fall along the way without endangering the entire effort.

This group of men came to be called the Forlorn Hope. As Captain J.J. Kellogg of the 113th Illinois remembered, nobody missed for a moment the unlikelihood of the Forlorn Hope's success. Especially telling was the fact that Major Generals Grant and Sherman had not simply assigned a group of men to the detail.

Not that the idea of having a "storming party" precede the attacking infantry regiments was up for negotiation. By Sherman's orders three men from each company must volunteer for the duty. This is an important distinction to note, as many are quick to assume that each man in the Forlorn Hope was either a super-patriot who willingly laid down his life for the great cause of the Union, or a super-optimist who believed the plan could work. Given the fact that each company had to cough up a quota of sacrificial lambs for Sherman's pet whim, it's more likely that many or most of the men who "volunteered" for the Forlorn Hope did so without any illusions that the foolhardy plan could work, or was worth dying for, but did so only to keep other men in their company from having to die for it themselves.

When the men in Kellogg's company were offered this "privilege," nobody volunteered at first, despite the promise of a 60-day furlough for anyone who stepped forward. Kellogg described the scene: "We looked into each other's faces for some seconds. We were speechless and felt a dread of what might develop. We knew that as a general thing the man who volunteers and goes into the storming party 'leaves all hope behind.' It means nearly sure death. . . .

"Finally there was a movement. Old Joe Smith, white headed, rough visaged and grizzled by the storms of a half century, stepped to the front and calling back to his bunkmate said, "Come on, Lish," and Elisha Johns filed out by his side. Then after a brief interval, Sergt. James Henry volunteered for the third place. Company B's quota was now complete, and those brave fellows hurried away to take their places in the ranks of the storming party."

Just before the Forlorn Hope began running for the salient, with the 30th Ohio a short distance behind them, Grant ordered the artillerists all around the siege area to open fire on the Confederates' mounted guns and parapets. The siege guns had been pounding all night, and now they returned, hoping to suppress the Rebels' fire long enough to allow the Forlorn Hope and the other assault brigades to do their work.

The results were as disastrous as you'd expect. Approaching at a dead run once it came out from behind the shelter of the road cut, the Forlorn Hope was met by a murderous barrage of musket fire. Only a handful of these men made it to the ditch before being cut down by musket fire. The few who made the ditch couldn't even begin to fill it in—not even with their bodies.

Company B's grizzled volunteer Joe Smith, however, never made it to the ditch—but this was a fortunate thing. "Pinned down" behind abatis,

"Lieut. Luther was shot by a rifle ball, hitting to the right of his mouth and passing out at the back of his neck. He was watching the effect of the shots of our Parrot guns on the rebel works at the time. He never spoke again, and died in about 20 minutes."
—**Captain Richard W. Burt, 76th Ohio Volunteer Infantry, Sunday, May 30, 1863**

"Today I heard some Yanks talking just outside our works, and I peeped over and saw a Yankee officer sitting with his back to me, about fifteen feet away, I could have easily shot his head off, but did not have the heart to do such an act, so I let him live. I believe he was a good man and the Lord protected him, and put it into my heart to spare his life."
—**William L. Truman, 1st Missouri Light Artillery, C.S.A. (Wade's Brigade), June 27, 1863**

A Guided Tour through History

Snipers

Snipers on both sides took the lives of many men, both North and South. From the Federals' advanced rifle pits—or, in the case of one sharpshooter from General John A. Logan's Division, from atop a tower made of railroad ties—Union snipers lay in wait at all times for a Confederate to expose himself. Generals Martin E. Green and Isham Garrott were both killed this way—along with countless other infantrymen. For much of the siege, each Federal infantryman was required to take a turn in the forward pits and fire off fifty shots. Some men admitted later that they often shot at nothing, simply to get their fifty rounds out of the way and escape back to the relative safety at the rear.

"One day we had to lay in rifle pits about three feet wide, three or more deep. I know I got awful tired so I got up and set on the ground that was taken out of the ditch. I did not set long till the Captain seen me. He yelled out get down there. You will get your head shot off. I just dropped down when zip came a bullet. To say I was scared is mild. I never after that exposed myself."

—**Diary of Private T.J. Moses, 93rd Regiment, Illinois Volunteers**

with his rifle barrel set conveniently in the crotch of a felled tree, Smith fired back at the Confederates. After the attacking regiments faltered and the assault collapsed, Old Joe staggered back to his company, where he found his bunkmate Elisha Johns had miraculously survived as well. As had Sergeant Henry.

While 85 percent of the Forlorn Hope had been killed or seriously injured, the three volunteers had not only kept their company mates from being killed, but astonishingly, they had avoided serious injury themselves. In the days that followed, as the rest of the company settled into the prolonged siege that would stretch on for forty-two hot and steamy days, all three of Company B's Forlorn Hopers headed home for well-deserved sixty-day furloughs.

The Confederates couldn't be quite as profligate with their ammunition, but they did manage to kill a number of the men digging the approach trenches, despite the sap rollers.

Tour Stop 8: The Surrender Interview Site

South of the 3rd Louisiana Redan, look for the sign labeled the surrender interview site, on your left off Pemberton Avenue. Park here, between the Union and Confederate lines. This is the spot—marked by the upside-down cannon, where General John C. Pemberton went at 3:00 p.m. on July 3 to discuss conditions of surrender. Pemberton had held a council of war with his generals, asking whether any of them thought—now that a rescue from General Johnston seemed unlikely—that their army could somehow effect a "breakout" through the Union lines. Brigadier General Stephen D. Lee wrote from Vicksburg on July 3, 1863, "I do not think it is time to surrender this garrison and post yet. Nor do I think it practicable to cut our way out. When it is time to surrender, the terms proposed by Grant are as good as we can expect. I still have hopes of Johnston relieving the garrison."

Lee, however, was quite alone in his optimism as regarded Johnston. The others all agreed that staying put was only an invitation to starvation and mutiny. With supplies and munitions critically low, and rumors afloat that Grant planned another massive assault within days—quite possibly on July 4—surrender or escape were the only alternatives. When Pemberton polled his generals as to the likelihood of a successful escape, General Carter Stevenson made it clear that a large number of his men, starving in their rifle pits for weeks, could never make it to the Big Black River—where the escaping army would have to cross, burning the bridges behind them. At least

10,000 of Pemberton's 30,000 men were far too sick, wounded, or starved to mobilize.

Finally, over General Stephen D. Lee's objections, on July 3, Pemberton sent Major General John S. Bowen—himself days away from death by dysentery—to talk to Grant. Bowen and Grant were friends from before the war, and Bowen figured he could get as good terms as anybody from the Union general.

In the message Bowen delivered to Grant, Pemberton postured a bit, hoping for good terms, claiming that although he felt himself "fully able" to hold his position "for a yet indefinite period," he was proposing a surrender interview to "save further effusion of blood, which must otherwise be shed to a frightful extent."

The letter Grant sent back with Bowen very nearly ended the truce: "The useless effusion of blood you propose stopping by this course can be ended at any time you may choose, by an unconditional surrender of the city and garrison . . . I do not favor the proposition of appointing commissioners to arrange the terms of capitulation, because I have no terms other than those indicated above."

Pemberton told Bowen that he had no intentions of surrendering unconditionally, and seeing the window of opportunity closing, Bowen told the whitest of lies: General Grant was amenable to sitting down to discuss the matter, he told his superior officer, if Pemberton was willing.

Assuming that Grant might be more reasonable in person than on official letterhead, Pemberton agreed to this meeting. At 3:00 p.m., Pemberton rode out to this site with Bowen and an aide.

Grant's transports running the batteries

Grant, having understood from Bowen that Pemberton was willing to discuss the logistics of his unconditional surrender, rode forward at 3:00 p.m. with two subordinates, and the two commanders sat down together beneath the shade of an oak tree at the spot where the cannon barrel now stands—midway between their armies' lines.

In the pause of hostilities between the two great armies, the oversized egos of Grant and Pemberton battled in their stead. Grant—who had snuffed and shattered so many of the soldiers' lives entrusted to him in repeated failed attempts to capture Vicksburg—wasn't about to let go of his "unconditional surrender" reputation now. Making compromise especially difficult for Grant was the fact that, from early on in the siege, long before hundreds of lives had been lost on the slopes of various redans and redoubts, Pemberton had offered Grant the chance to take the city, if only he'd allow Pemberton's army to march out, unmolested.

Grant had refused, and hence, arguably, much of the bloodshed of the following weeks lay on his shoulders. If he were to accept anything but an unconditional surrender now, the slaughter of recent weeks would enjoy not even the ghost of a justification.

On the other hand, Pemberton was already fighting the reputation, from his Charleston days, of being a lightweight without the resolve to hold an important position. Already suspected of disloyalty by many Confederates, he knew that his successfully protracted hold of the city would be heavily overshadowed by the city's ultimate fall into Union hands. What he wanted was some sort of concession from Grant—some admission that Pemberton's stubbornness had aided the Confederate cause is some concrete way.

Because of Bowen's machinations, Grant also arrived here on July 3 believing that Pemberton's agreement to meet signaled his willingness to unconditionally surrender his army. When the two generals began to talk and it became clear that this wasn't the case, and that Grant was unwilling to discuss any concessions, Pemberton shot a glare at Bowen. Then he turned to Grant and told him, "I can assure you, sir, you will bury many more of your men before you enter Vicksburg."

According to Pemberton, Grant at this point suggested that the two of them—old acquaintances from the Mexican War—sit off to the side and talk while their aides discussed the terms of surrender. And so, while Bowen and Pemberton's aide Louis M. Montgomery talked over terms with Union generals Andrew J. Smith and James McPherson, like two old veterans, Grant and

Pemberton sat here and discussed old times and mutual acquaintances.

Although they left the field that day after a brief exchange of notes, the commanders agreed upon the terms of surrender. The next morning, July 4, the Confederate defenders marched out of their forts and trenches, stacked arms, and were paroled. Vicksburg had fallen, but—thanks to Pemberton's obstinacy, and Grant's desire to avoid saddling his army with the responsibility of caring for 30,000 half-starved prisoners in enemy territory with Johnston on the prowl—the Confederates were issued paroles in which they promised not to fight against the United States until they had been formally exchanged for prisoners held by the Confederacy. Consequently, despite the glory heaped upon Grant after his army's conquest of Vicksburg, within months Grant's men would end up having to fight many of these same men again, farther east.

In this house on July 3, 1863, Pemberton met one last time in Council of War with his generals. With only General Stephen Lee dissenting, the men agreed that further resistance was futile.

"We have failed with heavy losses on our side, and indeed it is an almost if not entirely human impossibility to take this Fort from this side."
—**Private Gouldsmith D. Molineaux, 8th Illinois Volunteer Infantry**

The largest and most intimidating fortification in the Confederate defense, the Great Redoubt, was attacked on May 22, 1863, by Union General John Stevenson's brigade. Early that morning, twenty-eight-year-old Private Gouldsmith D. Molineaux wrote in his unpublished journal (now in possession of Augustana College), "This is a warm morning. We have drawn rations and are now preparing for the Charge. The Lord Almighty protect me. I put my trust in him alone now."

At 10 a.m., the charge began. The mostly Irish-immigrant 7th Missouri, flying an emerald battle flag, reached the walls of the Great Redoubt bearing ladders, with the order not to fire their guns until they had scaled the ladders and reached the top of the redoubt.

It was an unlikely plan—the idea that men clambering, one by one, up a handful of ladders could overwhelm hundreds of defenders was insanely optimistic. This point was made moot by the fact that the ladders the Union army provided the men were several feet too short to reach the top of the parapets.

Molineaux wrote, "Later, 10 A.M. All ready. Our Brigade is to go first in front, the 7th, MO Regt in advance of the Brigade and the 8th Ill next, 81st ILL & then 32nd Ohio."

Later that afternoon, from "behind a stump," safe from sniper fire, Molineaux described what had happened: "The Seventh Missouri made the charge, which we was to wait for orders to come on, but failed to get them as the 7th was almost annihilated. They carried the ladders right to the walls but there they laid them down or the carriers were shot & they fell back."

Later, Molineaux expressed his relief that his regiment had not been called to follow the 7th Missouri: "We have been under a scathing fire for several hours on getting our last position behind a hill, where we was to make our final charge and

Vicksburg Digs In

Vicksburgians had already weathered the bombardments of Admiral David Farragut's gunboats in the spring and early summer of 1862; at the beginning of the 1863 siege, the town's residents felt confident that this bombardment, too, would end quickly.

It wouldn't.

As shells of every description continued to batter the city, the people retreated to the hillsides, digging—or paying someone else to dig—cave dwellings in the area's thick, cohesive loess soil, which did not require shoring.

Mary Webster Loughborough experienced cave life firsthand after fleeing to Vicksburg from Jackson. She found shelter in a Vicksburg cave along with friends, her two-year-old daughter, and her Confederate officer husband.

In her memoir, *My Cave Life in Vicksburg,* Loughborough explained that while some of the caves were the simple, dark, cramped, hollowed-out places you'd expect, many Vicksburg shelters were surprisingly elaborate. Cave dwellers often furnished these shelters with beds, chairs, tables, carpets, and lots of candles, and carved out shelves for holding books and flowers. While most of the caves were designed for single families, some could hold as many as 200 people, with several entrances and passageways connecting larger rooms together.

With earthen "ceilings" often as thick as five feet, the caves were safer than the homes up on the surface, but not completely impervious to the Union's relentless shelling. Sometimes shells would make it into the doorways or through the ceiling of a cave.

Stuffy, damp, and claustrophobic, the hand-dug caves of Vicksburg nevertheless did what they were designed to do. When the bombardment finally ceased, the caves' relative security had spared the lives of all but a dozen or so Vicksburg residents.

scale the walls of their fort. We have ladders (2 to a Company); just think if one man to mount the ladder at a time."

After more fighting, late in the afternoon Molineaux again turned to his journal to reflect on the day's events: "It is now 5 p.m. We have gained this position and will probably hold it, 300 yds from the Enemy work, who are throwing shells & shot at us incessantly. We have lost many from the 8th in this scrape" [In the day's fighting, the 8th lost 4 enlisted men killed, 18 enlisted man and 1 officer wounded.] . . .

"This has been a severe day of heat. Several sunstrokes. . . . I fear many more brave lives will be here sacrificed as it were, before we are in possession of Vicksburg. It is a Gibraltar indeed."

After the second attack on the Stockade Redan, even Sherman and Grant had seen enough to realize that the Army of the Tennessee wasn't big enough to force the Confederates from Vicksburg. Hunger would have to do it.

"Sitting in the cave, one evening, I heard the most heartrending screams and moans. I was told that a mother had taken a child into a cave about a hundred yards from us; and having laid it on its little bed, as the poor woman believed, in safety, she took her seat near the entrance of the cave. A mortar shell came rushing through the air, and fell with much force, entering the earth above the sleeping child—cutting through into the cave—oh! most horrible sight to the mother—crushing in the upper part of the little sleeping head, and taking away the young innocent life without a look or word of passing love to be treasured in the mother's heart."
—**Mary Loughborough**

Tour Stop 10: Second Texas Lunette

Here you'll find your second chance to picnic on the park grounds.

The Second Texas Lunette guarded the Baldwin Ferry Road, which passed in front of this work before entering Vicksburg. On May 22, the Second Texas Volunteers who manned this fort fought off the fierce attacks of McClernand's men.

The 2nd Texas Lunette saw some of the fiercest fighting during the assaults of May 22.

Here after sending his men to slaughter—twice—on May 22, the chagrined Grant refused to request a temporary truce to allow his men to retrieve the dead and wounded Union men strewn about at the foot of Confederate parapets. Grant apologists suggest that Grant felt he would be showing a "sign of weakness" by requesting the truce—as if sending hundreds of men to be slain in suicidal charges had not been a sign of weakness in itself. Finally, on May 25, Pemberton himself sent a message to Grant requesting the truce "in the name of humanity." Grant acquiesced and a brief halt in hostilities allowed the Yankees to bury their dead and drag away any wounded who had managed to survive Grant's abandonment.

"Along the road [Baldwin Ferry] for more than 200 yards the bodies lay so thick that one might have walked the whole distance without touching the ground."
—**A Confederate officer, describing the May 22 assault**

"Oh the Horrors of this blood was to see the dead and dying—to see wounded after laying one day and night on the field with a wound in the arm or leg which, if cared for sooner, would of saved their lives, but after laying in the hot sun become all blowed with maggots rolling all over the wound since many such sights are to be seen."
—**William McCormick, 16th Ohio Volunteer Infantry, May 28, 1863**

Tour Stop 11: Railroad Redoubt

"Not ten rods from me was General Pemberton in all his splendor, calling to his retreating troops, saying: 'Go back to your works! There's only one line. We can whip them.'

Just at this moment they ran out a forty-eight pound gun about ten rods away, which was loaded with grape. It fired. One of these grape-shot struck me on the fourth rib on the right side and carried me over one hundred feet to the rear, dropping me into a canyon about fifty feet deep. . . . Had the second and third lines charged that day, it would have ended Vicksburg right there. We had them already beaten. But the rebels were able to drive back the front line, which charged alone, and the long siege of Vicksburg, lasting until July 4th, was the result."

—Corporal James Manley Sanford, 11th Wisconsin Volunteers

Park at the wide spot on the side of the road at NPS tour stop 13. Here's where the North came closest to breaching the Confederate defenses: the Railroad Redoubt. To get an idea of the shape of this irregular work, hold up your left hand in front of your face, turned in profile, as though you were going to karate chop the person in front of you. Tip it just a bit to the right, to the one o'clock position. Imagine these are the Confederate defensive lines in this section. Now bend your pointer finger forward as far as you can while keeping your thumb and other fingers vertical, until the tip of your pointer finger now points down and nearly into the heel of your palm. This was generally the shape of the Railroad Redoubt, and a good illustration of how it jutted out in front of the main Confederate line. Where you've parked is roughly beneath your finger's middle segment. Just where the park road swung right before you reached the parking area—that's the very tip of the finger, the southernmost and most exposed tip of the fort. It protruded some 150 yards from the main Confederate line.

Here, on this dangerous little peninsula, is where the men of the 30th Alabama Volunteer Infantry found themselves just before 10:00 a.m. on the morning of May 22, 1863. Beset for hours by heavy artillery fire, they had looked up from one particularly nasty barrage to find that the Yanks had blasted a hole in the parapet wall, right at the fingertip, or salient. Worse, most of the wall had tumbled outward, filling in the ditch beneath it, creating a perfect entry ramp for the invading Federals.

At 10:00 a.m., the guns suddenly silenced. Before the Alabamans could rebuild their wall, they saw hundreds of screaming bluecoats running for that opening. Worse, hundreds more were pouring past the tip on the left and right of the redan, threatening—if they successfully breached the wall further up the peninsula-shaped fortress—to cut the Alabamans off from the rest of the Confederates. As the Yanks reached the hole—mostly men of the 22nd Iowa, the Alabamans to either side of the opening fought hand to hand with the intruders.

There were too many of them. The Alabamans broke for the rear and the main Confederate line. A few fell back behind the traverses to provide cover fire—and finally, to hide. Some were taken prisoner by the Iowans, but most bolted successfully back to safety behind the main line, where their fellow Alabamans, the 86th Alabama, were pushing forward, firing at the dozen or so Yankees who had entered the fort—and at the 22nd Iowa's regimental colors, stabbed into the rampart.

Back to your left hand, where your pointer finger's middle segment meets the final segment, an interior traverse ran from the right side nearly to the left parapet wall—a perfect fallback position if the outer wall was breached. Some yards north of this, about halfway across your finger's middle section, stood another wall.

Before your finger cramps, let me finish the illustration. The railroad bed ran behind the redoubt. That's why the fort was here—to keep the Yankees from marching up the railroad tracks and into Vicksburg.

On the morning of June 22, the 30th Alabama Volunteers occupied the section represented by

"I would have written sooner but I hoped to be able by this time to inform you that Vicksburg had fallen and that we had again been the victors but alas my hopes have been disappointed and we are still battering away. . . ."
—**Private William J. Strofe, 48th Ohio Volunteers, June 7, 1863**

A Guided Tour through History

your finger's final segment, near your fingertip, facing east by northeast on their right and due south on the very tip.

Now remember, the rest of your hand, your other fingers, and your wrist, represent the main of the Confederate line—about 150 yards behind the southern tip of the redoubt. Obviously, the 30th Alabamans were in a very vulnerable spot, subject to attack from three sides. Hence, when two brigades of McClernand's men attacked all three sides of the fort at once, the Alabamans, after a fierce hand-to-hand tussle, fell back through behind the first traverse, the second traverse and back behind the main Confederate line. A handful were taken prisoner. The 86th Alabama and Waul's Texas Legion pushed back at the Federals, some of them taking positions behind the two internal fallback traverses, and successfully keeping all but a dozen or so of the Iowans outside the earthworks. Confederate rifle pits to the left and right of the peninsula-like tip of the redoubt poured enfilading fire on the Iowans inside.

The uniquely protruding nature of this work also meant that when the Yanks had chased out the Alabamans and captured the tip of the fort, McClernand could claim to have "captured the Rebel parapet" before him, but in doing so— implying that he had breached the Confederate lines—could well be considered an exaggeration. It was not unlike a country seizing Key West and claiming to have captured Florida.

Nonetheless, when the assault began at 10:00 a.m. on May 22, 1863, the 22nd Iowa did manage to take the tip of the fort (something of which Iowans are understandably proud; hence, the placement here of the Iowa Memorial.) As the Alabamans disappeared and the Iowans poured in, the Stars and Stripes indeed flew above the Railroad Redoubt. When McClernand heard about this, he wanted to send in more men to push further into the fort—but he had none to send. At 10:00 a.m. he had sent all of his brigades into battle, dividing them up between the Railroad Redoubt and the 2nd Texas Lunette to the north. He had no reserves, and the Iowans and other Federals who had now climbed into the fort were taking tremendous fire from Confederate muskets. Their hold on the redoubt was tenuous, at best, and it was only a matter of time until Pemberton sent reserves to run the Federals back out again.

Frantically, McClernand sent a messenger to General Grant, asking for reinforcements from McPherson's men, and for McPherson and Sherman to renew their attacks, keeping Pemberton's reserves dispersed across the whole 9-mile front.

Early in the afternoon, the commanding Confederate general on this stretch of the line—Brigadier General Stephen D. Lee (who was no blood relation to General Robert E. Lee) got word that although the assault as a whole had been "handsomely repulsed," the tip or "angle" of the fort had been breached and was being held by the Yankees. In his official report, Colonel T.N. Waul of Waul's Texas Legion explained what happened next: "Alive to the importance of the position, General Lee issued and reiterated orders to Colonel [C.M.] Shelley, commanding the Thirtieth Alabama, and Lieutenant-Colonel [E.W.] Pettus, commanding the Twentieth Alabama, to retake it at all hazards. Shelley called for volunteers to drive the Yankees

"General McClernand, instead of having taken any single point of the rebel main parapet, had only taken one or two small outlying lunettes open to the rear, where his men were at the mercy of the rebels behind their main parapet.
—**General William T. Sherman,** **Memoirs of General William T. Sherman**

from the fort—as well as the much larger number that had found shelter in the ditch to either side of the hole in the parapet." Captain H.P. Oden and Lieutenant William Wallis stepped forward, as did about fifteen men from the 30th Alabama, the regiment that had lost the fort in the first place.

When the men reached the first traverse, Oden saw a handful of other men from the 30th Alabama hiding behind the traverse wall. According to Waul, Oden called out to a Lieutenant Pearson, the ranking officer of these fugitives, "Why in the hell aren't you fighting?"

Pearson shouted back, "You won't be fighting long if you don't get in the trenches, and you'd better get there quick!"

Oden never got the chance. He immediately dropped, shot dead by a man from the 77th Illinois. A second later, a bullet tore into Lieutenant Wallis's back—Yankees who had bypassed the redoubt were now firing at it from the rear. More of the volunteers fell. The others turned and fled the way they'd come.

More attempts to retake the redoubt followed—none successful. Finally, the regiments refused to try another attack. Finally, around 5:30 p.m., General Lee directed the colonel of Waul's Texas Legion to take the fort. In his official report on the action, Waul explains what happened next:

He [Waul] immediately went, taking with him one battalion of the Legion to aid or support the assailants, if necessary, informing Captain [L.D.] Bradley and Lieutenant [J.] Hogue, who respectively commanded the companies that had been previously sent as a support to the garrison. These gallant officers not only willingly agreed, but solicited the honor of leading their companies to the assault, not wishing to expose a larger force than necessary. Captain Bradley was ordered to select 20 and Lieutenant Hogue 15 men from their respective companies. Lieutenant-Colonel [E.W.] Pettus, thoroughly acquainted with the locality and its approaches, came, musket in hand, and most gallantly offered to guide and lead the party into the fort. Three of Colonel Shelley's regiment also volunteered. With promptness and alacrity they moved to the assault, retook the fort, drove the enemy through the breach they entered, tore down the stand of colors still floating over the parapet, and sent them to the colonel commanding the Legion.

Waul's account of the Texans' retaking of the Railroad Redan is supported by other eyewitnesses.

Once the Yanks were driven from the fort, they hid in the ditch and fired at the Rebels from behind the parapet. Lee ordered two companies into the fort to get the Federals out of the ditch. Here the battle grew even more intense. The Rebels sweeping outside the parapet came under hot fire from those in the ditch as well as those elsewhere along the Union line. They fell back behind the parapets and harassed the Yanks with shells thrown as hand grenades. After dark, the Northerners slipped away, back behind their own lines.

Tour Stop 12: Cedar Hill Cemetery

To get to Cedar Hill Cemetery, 326 Lovers Lane, you'll either want to approach via downtown Vicksburg, or exit the park at the Fort Hill Road entrance, and, reach the cemetery at the corner of Sky Farm Road and Lovers Lane.

Unlike the high percentage of anonymous Union soldiers buried in the National Cemetery, most of the 5,000 Confederates here—roughly 15 out of every 16—were buried with name markers. Most were moved to the Soldiers Rest section of the cemetery from their original graves on the battlefield.

Here you'll find the graves of Confederate generals Martin L. Green, Isham Garrott, and John S. Bowen. Although Green and Garrott were killed in the line of battle, Bowen—after saving countless lives by brokering the surrender on July 3—died of dysentery in a stranger's farmhouse outside Edwards, Mississippi, on July 13. It was a tragic end, but the Irish-Catholic Bowen no doubt took some comfort in the presence of his wife and beloved priest Father John O'Bannon, known as "the fighting Chaplain of the Confederacy." O'Bannon would later that year be sent by Jefferson Davis to Rome on a secret mission to convince the Pope to recognize the Confederacy. Although he failed to convince the Vatican to break its previously stated neutrality concerning the war, O'Bannon did have success in his native Ireland, where his public speeches helped slow the number of Irish men who were immigrating to take up arms for the Union cause.

Tour Stop 13: Old Court House Museum

On July 4, 1863, Union troops marched unopposed into Vicksburg. The Stars and Stripes were run up the flagpole in front of the Warren County Courthouse for the first time since 1861, and a long, grim period of military occupation began for the people of Vicksburg.

With admirable consistency, however, the Union troops showed remarkable restraint over their victory. Colonel Joseph Stockton of the 72nd Illinois Infantry noted, "There were no cheers as we passed by these men, but the salutations were, 'How are you Yank?' 'How are you Reb?'"

A few days later, the Confederates would receive their paroles and head home to see their families until their exchanges came through and they were able to re-enlist with the Rebel army. Most of the Southern men who survived the defense of Vicksburg would, in fact, return to fight another day.

"Grant rode into the city this morning, with his staff, and a small body of troops, hauled down the beloved flag from the Court House, the only emblem of true and pure Democracy on earth today, and run up instead, a flag which we also once loved, when it represented the rights of the States, as guaranteed by the Constitution of the once United States. But today we hate that flag because it is the standard of government that has trampled under foot every right belonging to the Southern States."
—**William L. Truman, 1st Missouri Light Artillery, C.S.A., July 4, 1863**

Distinctively local, the Vicksburg Museum makes a great last stop on your tour.

"Afterward, no word of exultation was uttered to irritate the feelings of the prisoners. On the contrary, every sentinel who came upon post brought haversacks filled with provisions, which he would give to some famished Southerner, with the remark, "Here, reb, I know you are starved nearly to death."
—**Sergeant William Tunnard of the 3rd Louisiana**

"In our regiment was a boy who had a brother in the Rebel Army in Vicksburg. As we came to their works, the brother was there to meet the boy in our regiment. Our boy fell out of ranks, and they walked together, arms around each other's waists . . . the one in blue with uniform fresh, buttons shining, gun and bayonet bright; the other in gray, ragged uniform, barefoot and grimy. It was enough to make one feel sad that such things had to be."
—**Capt. Joel W. Strong, 10th Missouri Infantry**

Union soldiers broke into the stores of merchants who had been hoarding food and selling it at exorbitant prices to the starving civilians during the siege. By all accounts, they shared gladly with the starved Confederates and Vicksburg residents who crowded around them.

After the Fall

Despite the generosity and respect shown by the Federal troops at the surrender, life for civilians in Vicksburg was bitter and sometimes brutal. Though Grant immediately sent Sherman's and Ord's corps marching east to confront Johnston's army, McPherson's men stayed to hold and reinforce the defensive works the North had just spent forty-seven days trying to destroy. Such was war.

Grant quickly ordered many of the ill and injured (of both armies) upriver to Union hospitals, but those deemed unsalvageable were left to die at Vicksburg. Many men who technically survived the siege—by being alive on July 4, 1863—nonetheless died from wounds or illnesses contracted there.

For months afterwards, dying and desperately sick men of both armies overflowed the hospitals. At the same time, more than 25,000 emancipated slaves poured into "Freedom City," asking the Union army for protection and food. Grant initially appointed Major General John A. Logan military governor of Vicksburg, but before the month was out, Logan had headed back to his native Illinois at the behest of Abraham Lincoln, drumming up support for the Union cause and for the president's re-election. Many other Union officers would rule over Vicksburg during the remainder of the war;

least unpopular among them was probably Major General James McPherson, commonly singled out as the best of a bad lot.

As this 1864 photo gives evidence, after falling into Union hands, Vicksburg quickly regained its status as a bustling Mississippi River port.

The North's oppression of white Vicksburgians would continue through Reconstruction, leading to volatile racial tensions that in 1874 flared out into what was called the Vicksburg Massacre. Armed gangs of white Democrats struck throughout the city and surrounding area, resulting in the death of fifty and, by some estimates—as many as 300 African Americans in the Vicksburg area. President Ulysses S. Grant sent Federal troops to Vicksburg in January to stop the violence—but the return of martial law at the hands of their infamous "Conqueror" only brought about more resentment and racial division.

"The Yankees visited us today and we conversed freely and friendly together. We are treated with great hospitality by them."
—Private William Raleigh Clack, 43rd Tennessee Volunteers, July 5, 1863

The Old Court House Museum,
Vicksburg

So bitter was the memory of the period that
began on the humiliating day of July 4 of 1863 that
Vicksburg residents would not observe America's
birthday again until 1945, with many local sons
overseas fighting under the Stars and Stripes and
Harry S Truman, a Missouri Democrat, sitting in the
White House.

The Old Court House Museum today is a
touchingly old-fashioned museum that you'll
probably enjoy best at the end of your visit, when
you can make better sense of the items you'll see
displayed. Some of the more unique displays are
ones noting African Americans who fought for the
Confederacy and a display explaining the connec-
tion between Vicksburg, Theodore Roosevelt, and
the advent of the Teddy Bear.

Vicksburg: A Tourist's Guide to Exploring, Staying, and Eating

ENRICHING YOUR EXPERIENCE BEYOND THE BATTLEFIELD

Anchuca Historic Mansion, 1010 First East Street, (601) 661-0111, www.anchucamansion. com. A local politician built this mansion in 1830; its columns were added in 1847. Joseph Emory Davis, older brother to Confederate President Jefferson Davis, lived here until his death on September 18, 1870. After time in Federal prison, Jefferson Davis was able to reunite with his brother at the home in January 1869. Legend has it that he spoke from Anchuca's balcony, though some historians suggest that his speech mainly consisted of him apologizing that he could *not* address them, as that violated his parole and could get him re-arrested for treason. Nonetheless, whatever it was Jefferson Davis said from Anchuca's front balcony that day, folks agree that it was one of the last times the former Confederate president ever gave a speech in Vicksburg.

Though it houses both a superb B and B and restaurant, Anchuca is also worth touring in its own right. Call ahead for information.

Guided National Park tours, Vicksburg Convention and Visitors Bureau, 3300 Clay Street, (601) 636-0583 or (601) 636-3827, www.vicksburgcvb .org. The National Park provides licensed guides upon request (reservations recommended) who are experts on the park and can be a great addition to your experience—particularly for first-time visitors.

Tourists are not only welcome in Vicksburg—they're honored guests.

Tours are available during park hours. Fees start at $35 a car, more for larger vehicles.

Martha Vick House, 1300 Grove Street, (601) 638-7036, www.marthavickhouse.com. Open M–Sa 9–5, Su 1–5. Admission: $8.00; more than 10, $5.00; under 12, free. Built in 1830, this small, elegant home is the last remaining house from a member of the Vick family, the clan that gave the town its name.

McRaven Tour Home, 1445 Harrison Street, (601) 636-1663, www.mcraventourhome.com. Tours spring–fall, M–Sa 9–5, Su 10–5; closed in winter. Admission: adults $5.00; ages 12–17 $3.00; ages 6–11, $2.50; over 65, $4.50; Group rates are available. Caught in the crossfire during the assault on the Railroad Redoubt on May 22, 1863, the McRaven Home is also an interesting Southern manse in its own right, so much so that *National Geographic* called it "a time capsule of the South." The house was begun in 1797 as a Spanish Colonial, expanded in 1836 American Empire fashion, and renovated a third time in 1849 in the late Southern Greek Revival style. Today the home features three distinctly different sections, each furnished with antiques according to its period in time. Guided home tours last for an hour and a half. Ghost tours are also available—being that a field hospital was located on McRaven's grounds during the siege, it's perhaps no surprise that the home claims to be the most haunted house in Mississippi.

Vicksburg Battlefield Museum, 4139 North Frontage Road, (601) 638-6500, www.vicksburg-battlefieldmuseum.net. Open daily 9–5 daily.

Admission: students $3.25, adults $5.50; group rates available. The gunboat-shaped museum, just to the right of the National Park's main gate, is homegrown and heartfelt. For the Vicksburg novice, the extensive scale replica of the siege's various defensive works and attacks make it an extremely valuable place to visit.

WHERE TO STAY IN VICKSBURG

Vicksburg is located on I-20; consequently, you'll find an abundance of the usual chain hotels and motels near the freeway exits—but with the wealth of bed and breakfasts and inexpensive hotel rooms in the casinos down on the river below town, consider the chains your last resort.

The city's many bed and breakfasts offer an authentic nineteenth-century experience. These B and Bs are located in the city's historic district, so you'll stay in the same neighborhood where Vicksburg's noncombatants lived during the siege of 1863—when they weren't hunkered down in caves for safety. Some of the best are listed below.

Ahern's Belle of the Bends, 508 Klein Street, (601) 634-0737, (800) 844-2308, www.belleofthe-bends.com. Although it wasn't built until 1876, this very popular B and B and beautiful home reflects the sort of grandeur of antebellum Vicksburg, with its tree-shaded gardens, double verandas, and views of the river.

Anchuca Historic Mansion and Inn, 1010 First East Street, (601) 661-0111; (888) 686-0111, www.anchucamansion.com. The very first bed and breakfast in all of Mississippi, the Anchuca is also one of the oldest structures offering accommodations in Vicksburg. The building was begun about 1830 and completed in 1847. The Anchuca offers a large plantation-style breakfast.

Baer House Inn, 1117 Grove Street, (601) 883-1525, (866) 510-1525, www.baerhouseinn.ms. This 1870 Eastlake-style Victorian offers rooms with different themes, including the cheery Pineapple Room, the Mei Ling Mini Suite, and a quartet of *Gone With the Wind*–themed rooms: the Scarlett, the Rhett, the Tara, and the Bonnie Blue.

The Corners Mansion, 601 Klein Street, (601) 636-7421, (800) 444-7421. This Italianate and Classic Revival home near Baer House Inn was also built during Reconstruction. It features river views and offers a House on the Green for those seeking some privacy. The Corners also has rooms in the Quarters, a 1993 replica of the original house.

The **casino hotels** at the foot of the bluffs along the river—where the Confederate river batteries lay in 1863—offer another sort of memorable stay. Most provide little for children to do, other than swimming pools, but they usually feature family-style buffets—some of which are quite good—and nearly all offer riverfront views. (The notable exception is the Ameristar, which for some reason built its casino on the river and stuck its hotel across the road.) Of the various casino hotels, **Diamond Jacks** (3990 Washington Street, 877-711-0677, 601-636-5700, www.diamondjacks.com) is a good choice. Newly renovated, its large rooms have a Mississippi Riverfront motif.

WHERE TO EAT IN VICKSBURG

Because Vicksburg is a tourist destination, you'll find more good restaurants here than you might expect to find in a Mississippi town of this size. For families, it's hard to beat the all-you-can-eat buffets at the casinos along the river, of which the Ameristar—set inside an imitation riverboat—is my favorite. The list of suggestions below focuses on restaurants serving various types of Southern cuisine.

Café Anchuca, 1010 First East Street, (601) 661-0111, www.anchucamansion.com. Open Th–Sa 11–2 and 6–8, Su 11–2; closed M–W. Located at the Anchuca Mansion, this is a high-end restaurant, where the Shrimp Creole and salmon are great and the atmosphere is even better. Call ahead for reservations.

Goldie's Trail Bar-B-Que, 2430 South Frontage Road, (601) 636-9839. Open M–Th 11–9, F–Sa 11–10; closed Su. What Goldie's lacks in location—it's across I-20 from Vicksburg's historic district—it makes up for in good, no-nonsense barbecue.

Goldie's BBQ is a local favorite.

Students of the nation's various interpretations of the word "barbecue" will want to try Vicksburg's by ordering the sampler plate with the ribs, pulled pork, and sausage.

Gregory's Kitchen, 815 Highway 61 North, (601) 218-6075, www.gregoryskitchen.net. Open Th–Sa 5 p.m.–late, Su 11–2; closed M–W. A low-key locals' favorite over by the park on Highway 61, Gregory's all-you-can-eat catfish deal is cheaper and far more filling than what many local restaurants charge for a single serving—and it's also tastier than most. The coleslaw is superb. A Southern buffet is served on Sundays. Free Wi-Fi is available.

Rusty's Riverfront Grill, 901 Washington Street, (601) 638-2030, www.discoverourtown.com/webs/vicksburgms/rustys/. Open T–F 11–2 and 5–9:30, Sa 11–2 and 5–9:30; closed Su and M. A locals' favorite, Rusty's offers high-end, down-home food with an emphasis on fish. Specialties include seafood pasta with shrimp, crabmeat, and scallops in a lemon, butter, garlic, and wine sauce served over angel hair pasta. For an appetizer, try the fried green tomatoes topped with hollandaise sauce and lump crab.

Walnut Hills, 1214 Adams Street, (601) 638-4910, www.walnuthillsms.net. Open M–F 11–9, Su 11-2; closed on Sat. Set in a stately 1880 home on a residential street, Walnut Hills serves no breakfast but offers well-prepared family-style lunches (11–2), with à la carte service through dinner on weekdays. Unless you're on a serious diet—and are a person of deep integrity—Walnut Hills is the place you want to splurge and sample all the fine Southern cuisine. The fried chicken is excellent, but you already knew that, right? A favorite with locals and visitors alike, Walnut Hills is an essential Vicksburg dining experience.

Vicksburg

Walnut Hills provides family-style ("round table") service for lunch.

Glossary

abatis: Unsophisticated but not ineffective obstructions to slow and disrupt infantry assaults, normally made of felled trees with their branches sawed off, sharpened, and pointed towards the enemy; sometimes threaded with telegraph wire to make it even more entangling.

bombproof: A roofed dugout—sometimes a cave, sometimes a covered trench—meant to shelter soldiers from shrapnel, shot, and snipers.

C.S.A.: The Confederate States of America.

enfilading fire: Fire aimed at an enemy's sides (flanks) or rear.

firing step: Platform on which sharpshooters stood to fire under the head log.

flank: (noun) The side of a troop or cavalry formation—extremely vulnerable, since formations faced, and fired, forward. (verb) To maneuver one's unit, or oneself, to the side of the enemy with the purpose of firing on them.

gabions: Dirt-stuffed, bottomless, bullet-absorbing wicker baskets about 3 feet high and 2 feet in diameter, and weighing about 50 pounds. Used much as logs would be used in a parapet, to shield personnel and to reinforce earthen walls.

head log: Simply a log lain along the lip of a trench to protect men in the trench from being shot in the head by the enemy. The logs were elevated from the ground just enough to allow rifle barrels through them.

lunette: Two walls extending at right angles to the parapet walls and then meeting in a redan; the benefit of a lunette over a redan was that the lunette offered even more soldiers to line its walls and fire into the flanks and rear of attacking soldiers.

magazine: Any heavily fortified place used for storing munitions.

Minié ball: A muzzle-loading rifle bullet named for co-developer Claude Etienne Minié; more accurate, farther-traveling, and generally deadlier than round shot, it came into widespread use during the American Civil War.

parapet: An earth and log wall, normally a minimum of 8 feet high from the attacker's side, and often several feet higher.

position tablet: It looks like a metal plaque to you and me, but Vicksburgians have long called the alternately Blue (Union) and Red (Confederate) signs on the battlefield "position tablets."

redan: A pair of walls that jut out from the defensive line and meet at a 60-degree angle. These fang-shaped protrusions, lined with soldiers, allowed defenders the opportunity to fire into the flanks of attacking enemy formations.

redoubt: A freestanding, four-sided fortification set forward of the main defensive line, allowing prime opportunity for flanking attackers.

salient: The point where the walls of a redan meet. Typically, this was considered the weakest—that is, most easily overpowered—point in a redan, since the men further along the widening walls of the V could not fire at attackers approaching the salient without shooting their fellow soldiers.

sap: A 6-foot-deep, 8-foot-wide trench dug to provide safe travel from snipers for infantrymen and artillerists moving to and from the front lines, which grew increasingly closer to the enemy fortifications as the saps progressed. Saps were dug in a zigzagging fashion to keep artillerists and snipers from gaining an advantageous angle on the men in the saps.

sap roller: Made from the chassis of a railroad cart and piled high with gabions or cotton bales to protect the engineers and "pioneers" digging at the front of the trench.

traverse: Interior walls within a battery fortification meant to minimize the damage from exploding bombs, missiles, and guns.

trench: A ditch deep enough so that men could stand fully erect without being exposed to enemy fire.

Bibliography

Balfour, Emma H. *Mrs. Balfour's Civil War Diary: A Personal Account of the Siege of Vicksburg*. Vicksburg, Miss.: Old Courthouse Museum, 2008.

Cotton, Gordon A., and Jeff T. Giambrone. *Vicksburg and the War*. Gretna, La.: Pelican Pub. Co., 2004.

Crummer, Wilbur F. *With Grant at Fort Donelson, Shiloh and Vicksburg*. Whitefish, Mont.: Kessinger, 2008.

Foote, Shelby. *The Beleaguered City: The Vicksburg Campaign, December 1862–July 1863*. New York, N.Y.: Modern Library, 1995.

Grant, Ulysses S. *Memoirs and Selected Letters: Personal Memoirs of U.S. Grant, Selected Letters 1839–1865*. New York, N.Y.: Library of America, Distributed to the trade in the U.S. and Canada by Viking Press, 1990.

Hobbs, Charles A. *Vicksburg: A Poem*. Chicago, Ill.: Fairbanks & Co., 1880.

Hoehling, A.A. *Vicksburg: 47 Days of Siege*. Mechanicsburg, Pa.: Stackpole Books, 1996.

Kellogg, John Jackson. *War Experiences and the Story of the Vicksburg Campaign from "Milliken's Bend" to July 4, 1863;* being an accurate and graphic account of campaign events taken from the diary of Capt. J.J. Kellogg, of Co. B 113th Illinois Volunteer Infantry. Self-published, 1913

Logan, John Alexander. *The Great Conspiracy: Its Origin and History, A History of the Civil War in the United States of America.* Grand Rapids, Mich.: Kessinger, 2004.

Loughborough, Mary. *My Cave Life in Vicksburg.* Carlisle, Mass.: Applewood Books, 2001.

Pemberton, John C. *Pemberton, Defender of Vicksburg.* Chapel Hill, N.C.: The University of North Carolina Press, 2002.

Schulze, Bruce, ed. "The Siege of Vicksburg," *The Vicksburg Campaign Photo Album,* www.civilwaralbum.com/vicksburg/index.htm.

Sherman, William T. *Memoirs of General William T. Sherman.* New York, N.Y.: Da Capo Press, 1984.

Tunnard, William H. *A Southern Record: The History of the Third Regiment, Louisiana Infantry.* New York, N.Y.: Scholarly Office, University of Michigan Library, 2005.

Twain, Mark. *Life on the Mississippi.* New York, N.Y.: Modern Library, 2002.

Warren, Andrea. *Under Siege! Three Children at the Civil War Battle for Vicksburg.* New York, N.Y.: Farrar, Straus and Giroux, 2009.

Winschel, Terrence J. *Triumph and Defeat: The Vicksburg Campaign.* New York, N.Y.: Savas Beatie, 2004.

Index

Italicized page references indicate illustrations.

Vicksburg

Vicksburg